MINISTRY AND PRIESTHOOD

D0589094

WITHDRAWN
FOR SALE
LINCOLNSHIRE
COUNTY COUNCIL

AD 03238359

SERIES EDITORS: Leslie J Francis and Jeff Astley

MINISTRY AND PRIESTHOOD

Alastair Redfern

DARTON·LONGMAN+TODD

L·83

First published in 1999 by
Darton, Longman and Todd Ltd
1 Spencer Court
140-142 Wandsworth High Street
London SW18 4JJ

© 1999 Alastair Redfern

ISBN 0-232-52339-8

The right of Alastair Redfern to be identified as the author of this work has been
asserted in accordance with the Copyright, Designs and Patents Act 1988.

A catalogue record for this book is available from the British Library.

Designed by Sandie Boccacci
Phototypeset in Minion by Intype London Ltd
Printed and bound in Great Britain by
Page Bros, Norwich, Norfolk

CONTENTS

PREFACE

At the beginning of the third millennium a new mood is sweeping through the Christian churches. This mood is reflected in a more radical commitment to discipleship among a laity who wish to be theologically informed and fully equipped for Christian ministry in the secular world.

Exploring Faith: theology for life is designed for people who want to take Christian theology seriously. Taken seriously, Christian theology engages the mind, involves the heart, and seeks active expression in the way we live. Those who explore their faith in this way are beginning to shape a theology for life.

Exploring Faith: theology for life is rooted in the individual experience of the world and in the ways through which God is made known in the world. Such experience is related to and interpreted in the light of the Christian tradition. Each volume in the series takes a key aspect of theology, and explores this aspect in dialogue with the readers' own experience. Each volume is written by a scholar who has clear authority in the area of theology discussed and who takes seriously the ways in which busy adults learn.

The volumes are suitable for all those who wish to learn more about the Christian faith and ministry, including those who have already taken Christian basic courses (such as *Alpha* and *Emmaus*) and have been inspired to undertake further study, those preparing to take theology as an undergraduate course, and those already engaged on degree programmes. The volumes have been developed for individuals to work on alone or for groups to study together.

Already groups of Christians are using the *Exploring Faith: theology for life* series throughout the United Kingdom, linked by an exciting initiative pioneered jointly by the Anglican dioceses, the Board of Education of the Church and World Division and the Ministry Division of the Archbishops' Council of the Church of England, the National

Society and the Church Colleges. Used in this way each volume can earn credits towards one of the Church Colleges' Certificates and provide access to degree level study. Further information about the Church Colleges' Certificate Programme is provided on page 130.

The Church Colleges' Certificate Programme integrates well with the lifelong learning agenda which now plays such a crucial role in educational priorities. Learning Christians can find their way into degree-bearing programmes through this series *Exploring Faith: theology for life* linked with the Church Colleges' Certificates.

In preparing a series of this kind, much work is done behind the scenes. Financial and staff support have been generously given by the Ministry Division. Thanks are due to Marilyn Parry for the vision of bringing together the Aston materials and the Anglican Church Colleges of Higher Education. Thanks also should go to the Aston staff and the original authors for being willing to make the materials available for reworking. We are also grateful for financial support from the following Church Colleges: Chester College; Christ Church University College, Canterbury; The College of St Mark and St John, Plymouth; St Martin's College, Lancaster; Trinity College Carmarthen; and Whitelands College (Roehampton Institute). Without the industry, patience, perception, commitment and skill of Ruth Ackroyd this series would have remained but a dream.

The series editors wish to express their personal thanks to colleagues who have helped them shape the series identity, especially Diane Drayson, Ros Fane, Evelyn Jackson, Anne Rees and Morag Reeve, and to the individual authors who have produced high-quality text on schedule and so generously accepted firm editorial direction. The editorial work has been supported by the North of England Institute for Christian Education and the Centre for Theology and Education at Trinity College Carmarthen.

Leslie J Francis
Jeff Astley

INTRODUCTION

This book is not designed to be simply read through: it needs to be worked through. The ideas, experiences and aspirations of the reader are an essential ingredient and need to be put into dialogue with the material in each chapter.

The aim is not to give 'answers' but to offer suggestions, some of them deliberately unfashionable, drawing upon the insights of previous ages alongside those of contemporary thinkers and documents. In reaction to this material you are invited to explore vocation, ministry and the priesthood of all believers. No one can be a solitary Christian, since faith puts us into deeper relationship with God and with all of God's creation. The outworking of the faith of any individual needs to be explored within this larger context.

As Christians enter a new millennium there is a vigorous debate about ministry and priesthood which reflects some of the major tensions in western culture between:

- the rights and needs of individuals and the place of institutions;
- aspirations for equality and the continuing realities of hierarchy;
- the desire for local or regional recognition and the processes of globalisation.

The format of the book invites individuals or study groups to put their own ideas and experiences regarding ministry and priesthood over against the insights of a variety of thinkers and traditions. Out of this process can come an appreciation of the wider framework within which such exploration should take place and the opportunity to evaluate some of the current debate in the churches about this particular agenda.

The book invites you to begin by crystallising your own current experience of ministry and priesthood, using the Ministry Questionnaire. This document then becomes a key reference point for further exploration and evaluation.

The process of the book moves from a consideration of your own ideas to a broader engagement with key issues in this whole area, including the relationship of ministry and priesthood and the nature of public representative ministry.

There follows a chapter outlining something of the historical and doctrinal background, which provides a framework for assessing the contemporary debates about ministry and priesthood and their significance for Christian discipleship and church life.

A separate chapter on women and ministry uses a case study of a colourful character, Maude Royden, to highlight some of the basic issues and to provide a sharp challenge to our tendency to feel that significant progress has been made in this crucial area.

Subsequent chapters explore the place of order and authority, and of the catholic and the local. There is an important debate about the place of structures and stability in a pluralistic culture which exalts individual rights and opportunities while being suspicious of institutions and hierarchy. Historically churches have seen institutional life as prior and primary, but much contemporary discussion of ministry and priesthood involves recognition that in our own times it is the uniqueness of each individual that is taken to be the essential factor. This is evident in the theology and the practice of most contemporary churches.

This agenda is explored from another perspective by examining the teaching of Evelyn Underhill regarding the spirituality of ministry and priesthood.

The final chapter uses material from two distinguished contemporary writers in order to test out current debate and possibilities.

If Christians are to offer a credible witness in the modern world, then each believer needs to work hard at clarifying what their own particular ministry might be and how that contribution can best fit into the life of the wider church. This book offers a structure within which such ecumenical exploration can take place, drawing on the author's personal experience shaped within an Anglican context.

1. MARKS OF MINISTRY: THE CALL TO BE ME

Introduction

This chapter invites you to identify your own initial thoughts about ministry and priesthood, and to place these within the context of your experience of your local church.

There are no neat definitions provided for the terms 'ministry' and 'priesthood': one of the aims of this book is to introduce you to the lively debate about how these words have been understood in the past and how we might best use them today.

Reflecting on experience
📖 **Complete the Ministry Questionnaire (see Appendix).**

If you are reading this book as part of a group, compare your answers with those of others in the group. If you are studying on your own, ask one or two other people to complete the same questionnaire and then compare the results.

Make a note of issues or areas where there might be a range of views.

Christian initiation

God has called you by name, and made you His own.

These words from the modern initiation rite in the Church of England (1998) emphasise the uniqueness of each person and the fact that the gift of life imposes responsibilities, most especially:

- to acknowledge God as Father, Son and Holy Spirit (Creator, Redeemer, Sustainer); this is focused in baptism;
- to play an appropriate part within the body of Christ.

The modern initiation rite also contains the following Prayer of Commission:

> Those who are baptised are called to worship and serve God.
>
> Will you continue in the apostles' teaching and fellowship,
> in the breaking of bread, and in the prayers?
> **With the help of God, I will.**
>
> Will you persevere in resisting evil,
> and, whenever you fall into sin, repent and return to the Lord?
> **With the help of God, I will.**
>
> Will you proclaim by word and example
> the good news of God in Christ?
> **With the help of God, I will.**
>
> Will you acknowledge Christ's authority over human society,
> by prayer for the world and its leaders,
> by defending the weak, and by seeking peace and justice?
> **With the help of God, I will.**
>
> May Christ dwell in your hearts through faith,
> that you may be rooted and grounded in love
> and bring forth the fruit of the Spirit.
> **Amen.**

The Porvoo Common Statement between the British and Irish Anglican Churches and The Nordic and Baltic Lutheran Churches (Council for Christian Unity, 1993) makes a similar point:

> We believe that *all members of the Church* are called to participate in its apostolic mission. All the baptised are therefore given various gifts and ministries by the Holy Spirit. They are called to offer their being as 'a living sacrifice' and to intercede for the Church and the salvation of the world. This is the corporate priesthood of the whole people of God and the calling to ministry and service (1 Peter 2:5).

EXERCISE
📖 **Read 1 Corinthians 12.**

What does this passage say to you about ministry? Make notes of your initial reflections.

Christian ministry

In a book of essays entitled *All Are Called* (General Synod Board of Education, 1985), there was an attempt to highlight a check-list of some of the things involved in the idea of ministry. Ministry involves many areas.

In our daily work, ministry can involve:
- exercising ministry in our place of work;
- relating our faith to the world of work.

In politics, ministry can involve:
- being involved in local or national politics;
- campaigning for justice and peace.

In the community, ministry can involve:
- taking a part in the life of our street and neighbourhood;
- arranging a community project.

In the family, ministry can involve:
- giving time to my family.

In areas of service, ministry can involve:
- representing the church on local projects and charities;
- co-operation with other churches.

In pastoral care, ministry can involve:
- visiting the sick, the bereaved, the housebound;
- organising a good-neighbour scheme.

In worship, ministry can involve:
- leading worship or preaching, leading prayers or doing readings;
- music;
- special services;
- prayer groups.

In teaching, ministry can involve:
- work with children or Sunday School;
- work with teenagers pre- or post-confirmation;
- adult confirmation preparation;

- marriage preparation or preparation of families for baptism;
- leading house-groups.
  In 'spreading the news', ministry can involve:
- sharing our faith with others;
- parish magazine writing or editing or distribution.
  In administration, ministry can involve:
- church or churchyard cleaning, catering, PCC, churchwarden duties;
- typing or printing or secretarial work or staffing the parish office.
  In fellowship, ministry can involve:
- helping to build community and welcoming newcomers;
- events and social activities.

EXERCISE

How do you react to this check-list? Is there anything important missing? Place the list in order of priority.

How would you express your own understanding of ministry in relation to this check-list and the Porvoo Statement?

The scope and style of ministry

Some lines from the following poem by Evelyn Underhill, called *Immanence*, illustrate one view of ministry.

> I come in the little things,
> Saith the Lord:
> Not borne on morning wings
> Of majesty, but I have set My Feet
> Amidst the delicate and bladed wheat
> That springs triumphant in the furrowed sod.
> There do I dwell, in weakness and in power;
> Not broken or divided, saith our God.

EXERCISE

What might this poem teach us about the scope and style of Christian ministry?

Whose ministry and what ministry?

In *The Alternative Service Book 1980* of the Church of England the collect used at the beginning of a service to commission new ministry reads as follows:

> God our Father, Lord of all the world,
> We thank you that through your Son
> You have called us into the fellowship
>   of your universal Church:
> hear our prayer for your faithful people
> that each in their vocation and ministry
> may be an instrument of your love ...

The prayer goes on to focus on the particular ministry to be inaugurated.

In this prayer we have a clear articulation of the fact that call and commission to ministry comes from God, who gives each person 'their vocation and ministry'.

Hence ministry is not simply a matter of our choosing, it is primarily about how we discern the call of God and then receive grace to fulfil that calling. Ministry comes out of discerning vocation. One of the great themes of scripture is that discernment is not always obvious or straightforward: 'vocation and ministry' tend to emerge from a struggle between our human, superficial, view of life in this world, and God's more profound way of working. The final part of this chapter is designed to help you begin to think about this important perspective on the whole subject of ministry and priesthood.

EXERCISE
📖 **Read the Book of Ruth.**

Make notes of your reflections about the nature of vocation and ministry in this book.

The Book of Ruth comes between the Book of Judges and the Books of Samuel and Kings, all of which are concerned with great public events in the story of the people of Israel. Ruth reminds us that alongside public life there is a key place for the small scale, the individual, and the facing of domestic and personal issues. We shall explore the themes of vocation and ministry in Ruth, and the mystery that in the call of apparently ordinary people to discipleship, something significant can be achieved: in this case a key stage in the line which is to produce the great King David. The call and commission of anyone can be pregnant with possibilities for God's new life to grow and for God's Kingdom to be advanced, often without those involved recognising the fact. Yet each has a part to play.

The person we will consider in detail from the Book of Ruth is her mother-in-law, Naomi.

EXERCISE

How does Naomi discover who she is called to be? How does she discover what she is called and commissioned to contribute?

Here are some features of the story for consideration:
1. Naomi needs to move away from her home, from the place where she feels settled and safe, in order to see things differently: in order to get a different perspective and thus be able to play her allotted part in the bearing of God's new life.
2. She goes to Moab because of famine and economic necessity. God often works through material circumstances.
3. At first her vocation and ministry seems clear: to raise a family in Moab and make a new life there.
4. However, as so often in scripture, there is a major setback. She loses her husband and sons. She loses her food supply. Famine comes again. The first call to ministry has been a false start. It is not as simple as it seems.
5. She is led to feel that she should return home. Her real ministry is in fact to be in a place she knows already. Vocation, the call to ministry, is rarely a steady progress to somewhere completely new. Often it involves honouring what has already been given. Another example would be Moses, who was trained for leadership at the court of Pharaoh, left that life, but then had to recognise a call to leadership of the people.
6. When Naomi returns to Bethlehem she recognises that she has become a different person: 'My name now is Mara' (bitter). It is a tough lesson to learn, that vocation is often realised close to where

God has placed us but in a very different way from what we first believed.

7. Ruth is given an active ministry when they are hungry. Ruth is sent to glean in the fields while Naomi has to stay at home, helpless, prayerful, depending on someone else to play a part in helping her discover her own call and commission. This is one of the hardest lessons of all.

8. Out of this period of waiting and worrying, while Ruth and Boaz play active roles, comes the marriage of Naomi's daughter-in-law to her kinsman, and the birth of the baby Obed. The women of Bethlehem say to Naomi, 'Here is your son.' New life has come to her in Bethlehem, the place where God's new life is born on earth. For each of us the consideration of a call to ministry will involve identifying our own Bethlehem, the place where God's life can most fruitfully be born for the well-being of God's Kingdom.

9. More challenging still is the fact that this new life, which it has been Naomi's ministry to foster and now nourish, is not the 'pure' Jewish life she might have expected. A key element has been her ability to include a Moabite woman, someone normally considered to be of no significance to the public outworking of God's Kingdom on earth.

10. All this comes to fruition at harvest time. There is a harvest for every call to ministry:
    - it involves learning a new perspective, like a seed plunging into the darkness of the soil;
    - it includes the disintegration of our initial thoughts and aims;
    - it requires others to play their parts: it is not a simple transaction between the individual and God;
    - it contains an element of waiting and worrying;
    - it brings new life and new possibilities as sheer gift;
    - it depends on a relationship with those normally considered to be unsuitable for direct involvement in making the Kingdom.

Call to ministry

In this story of Naomi there are important issues regarding the call to ministry.

Continuity: Naomi comes back to be the person she was originally made to be, just as Paul, despite his dramatic conversion, remained the same energetic, aggressive, combative person. The call to ministry involves continuity, not a change to become a totally different person. In our modern world, where 'progress' is such a dominant theme, there is magnification of the human tendency to believe that the grass is always greener somewhere else. Naomi challenges us to look nearer home for clues about ministry.

Patience: Often God seems to work slowly or indirectly. Because we know the happy ending of this story we should not forget the terrible anguish of waiting, not knowing, fearing, praying. That must have been a large part of Naomi's journey to perceiving her real ministry. We are too easily dominated by 'goals' in considering ministry as a baptised person. The struggle and the waiting are equally important. God's timing requires our attentiveness and a faith that, however dark things seem, there is always more to come.

Bereavement: New life comes through loss: of familiar props and of familiar people. What is important for Naomi is that she can express her bitterness and frustration. Jesus says that if we follow him we will carry a cross. That is something Naomi was able to own.

Interdependence: Naomi could only fulfil her particular calling by working with, and giving space to, others. Ministry is never isolating, rather it puts us in deeper relationship with others. That is one of the lessons from the passage in 1 Corinthians 12.

Faithfulness: We must continue to trust in God and in others, however forsaken or unfulfilled we seem to feel. God could produce a 'son' for Naomi, after the death of her own sons, through a Moabitess.

Passivity: There is a place for being passive, as well as being active, both in the discernment and in the practice of ministry.

EXERCISE
📖 **Re-read the Book of Ruth.**

What can you learn about vocation and ministry from the stories of Ruth and Boaz respectively? ▶▶

Similarly, what can you learn about vocation and ministry from the stories of Mahlon, Chilion and Orpah? To what extent will much of what we call 'ministry' be essentially hidden from the public realm?

How do your reflections relate to the poem *Immanence*?

What do you think?

Here are some further issues for consideration:

1. What are the different roles you can discern in this story? Could they be described in terms of 'ministries'?
2. Do you have any reflections on the quotation from the Porvoo Common Statement in the light of this reading of Ruth?
3. Does everyone have a 'ministry' which is active and visible to any observer of the unfolding of God's call and purposes?
4. Is 'ministry' always a calling to something active and visible? How else can there be a calling to be 'an instrument of God's love'?

Further reading

Countryman, L W (1999), *Living on The Border of the Holy*, Wilton, Connecticut, Moorhouse.

Dewar, F (1991), *Called or Collared*, London, SPCK.

General Synod Board of Education (1985), *All are Called*, London, Church House Publishing.

Green, L (1987), *Power to the Powerless*, London, Marshall Pickering.

Greenwood, R (1996), *Practising Community*, London, SPCK.

Macquarrie, J (1972) *The Faith of the People of God*, London, SCM.

Tiller, J (1987) *The Gospel Community*, London, Marshall Pickering.

Tiller, J (1993), *Together in Mission and Ministry*, London, Church House Publishing.

2. PASTORAL AND PRIESTLY MINISTRY

Introduction

We have explored something of the relationship between vocation and ministry. Each human creature is born with the potential to become a particular kind of person, making a specific and unique contribution to the unfolding story of creation and salvation. But in the mystery of this life we cannot always see the path ahead clearly. Vocation, calling by God, requires us to discern that call, to pay attention: in private prayer, in public worship, in reflection on life in the world. Much can distract or mislead us. Thus vocation involves struggle, discernment and an ever-unfolding scenario, for each of us, for our families, groups, churches, nations, planet.

The outworking of the 'call' is what Christians designate as ministry.

Reflecting on experience
Think of an occasion on which you have tried to help someone in particular need:
- What did you try to do or say?
- What motivated you to try to help?
- What was the outcome for the person concerned?
- Can you describe your approach and your actions in terms of Christian ministry?

Definitions

In *A New Dictionary of Christian Theology* (Richardson and Bowden, 1983) the following definition is offered:

Christian ministry is a ministry of salvation in the service of the world. It originates in the charge given by Christ to the Church to carry out his ministry. All baptised are called to share in his service in accordance with their states of life, special gifts and roles within the structure of stable Christian community.

It is important to note that in this definition ministry is seen as:
- 'service of the world';
- being 'of salvation';
- rooted in the 'charge of Christ';
- involving 'all baptised';
- based in 'the structure of stable Christian community'.

All of these features point to the fact that for Christians, 'ministry' involves giving clearer focus and expression to the life-giving grace of God in creation, and in this sense it is 'priestly', participating in the mystery of Christ, his living, dying and rising again. Hence the Porvoo Common Statement (Council for Christian Unity, 1993) already referred to in chapter 1 states that:

> We believe that all members of the church are called to participate in its apostolic mission. All the baptised are therefore given various gifts and ministries by the Holy Spirit. They are called to offer their being as 'a living sacrifice' and to intercede for the Church and the salvation of the whole world. This is the corporate priesthood of the whole people of God and the calling to ministry and service.

Here is the basis of the 'priesthood for all believers', being the foundation of all Christian ministry.

EXERCISE

Look at your answers to question 3 of the Ministry Questionnaire which you completed as part of the work for chapter 1. Make brief notes in answer to the following questions:
- Are the key tasks and functions of your local church its primary 'vocation'?
- How do the responsibilities of your local church relate to the vocation and ministry of individual members?
- What highlights and maintains a sense of 'the priesthood of all believers'?   ▶▶

- How do individuals learn to discern their own particular vocation and ministry?
- How is the ministry of individual church members and of the local church community related to the needs and concerns of those amongst whom you all live and work?

Ministry in pride and prejudice

We are going to explore the notion of the priesthood of all believers and the outworking of vocation and ministry in this context, by examining the novel *Pride and Prejudice* written by Jane Austen and published in 1813.

If you have time you might like either to read the novel or to watch the 1995 video of the BBC adaptation of this story. Jane Austen's story provides an interesting insight into ministry and the priesthood of all believers at a time when the churches seemed to be struggling, and clergy were often seen as corrupt or incompetent. The author was the daughter of a clergyman and thus had first-hand experience of church life in a variety of communities.

In one of her letters describing her own work she comments that 'the thing to work on is three or four families in a country village'. This was not only a recipe for a good novel, it was also a structure whereby, within the novel, the priesthood of all believers, the outworking of Christian vocation and ministry, could be practised realistically and effectively.

Within the world of eighteenth-century England which she portrays, there are three key ingredients from the point of view of Christian ministry and priesthood. First, there is a tradition of high aspiration for the triumph of goodness, love, patience, joy, peace. These are based upon the life of the church, the teaching of scripture, the uncertainty of human life and the desire for fulfilment, now and in eternity. The second ingredient is a living community which aspires to these things in a mixed way, and with varying degrees of seriousness. Third, there are key people who help the living community relate better to the high aspirations which are latent in most and actual in some. This is the area of ministry and priesthood.

The novel *Pride and Prejudice* is the story of Mr and Mrs Bennett and their five daughters. They have no male heirs and thus on the death of

Mr Bennett, the property will pass to their cousin, Mr Collins, who is a clergyman.

The novel begins:

> It is a truth universally acknowledged, that a single man in possession of a large fortune must be in want of a wife.

This is a summary of the story: security and salvation for five daughters would be seen in terms of satisfactory marriages. This becomes a parable for the fact that for all human beings security and salvation come through stable relationships within a community. These provide the basis for the fullest flowering of goodness, love, patience, joy and peace, and a hopeful context within which human frailty and mortality can be held and nourished for eternity.

During the course of the novel, three of the Bennett girls find husbands: Jane, the eldest, Elizabeth, next eldest and her father's favourite, and Lydia, youngest and wildest of the girls. Jane and Elizabeth meet their eventual husbands through local society, Lydia through the military camp stationed for a time in the neighbourhood.

Alongside these three 'paths to salvation' is the story of Mr Collins, who is portrayed as a fawning, incompetent and unattractive clergyman, besotted with the privilege of ministering to his patron, Lady Catherine de Bourgh, and eventually marrying Elizabeth's friend Charlotte Lucas, a match of convenience in contrast to the three 'love' matches of the Bennett girls.

The story explores the rocky path to salvation for each of the three girls, with many upsets and disappointments along the way. Despite the clear public desire in that society for goodness, love, patience, joy and peace, it becomes obvious that all the characters fall short and make serious misjudgements of opinion and action: pride and prejudice so easily triumph over higher aspirations. Each character struggles to discover their vocation, some consciously measuring their path by the aspirations of a Christian society, others following more immediately selfish paths.

Ministry and humanity

Various characters illustrate the fallibility and failings, as well as the innate goodness, in humanity:

- Mr Bennett: kind but cynical, keen to limit his own responsibilities;
- Mrs Bennett: loud and coarse but deeply motivated by parental concern for her brood;

- Mr Collins: pompous, fawning, ambitious, symbol of the established Church;
- Mr Darcy: proud, insensitive, yet eager to be truthful and to follow his heart;
- George Wickham: an army officer with an eye for the main chance;
- Lydia Bennett: young, impetuous, she elopes with Wickham;
- Jane Bennett and Mr Bingley: both good people trapped by convention and pride and needing help to follow their vocation to marry;
- Elizabeth Bennett: the heroine, lively and active, keen to pursue goodness but capable of serious errors of judgement (pride and prejudice) which nearly wreck the fulfilment of her own vocation to marry Mr Darcy.

In this brief snapshot we see something of the mix which makes up human life. The novel follows the stories of a few families as their members struggle with the issue of vocation and ministry, and with the questions:

- Who am I supposed to be becoming?
- How should I best serve myself and others?

All the characters are flawed, especially Mr Collins who represents the institutional church and the formal priesthood. Yet each is struggling in various ways to recognise and pursue the high aspirations of that society for salvation through settled and secure relationships.

Elizabeth Bennett makes serious errors of judgement and needs the hand of providence to help open her eyes through a series of apparently chance encounters, so that her own vocation and those of her sisters can be fulfilled. But Elizabeth is blessed in this way and can thus help bring blessing to others, because whatever her mistakes or setbacks she consistently seeks to pursue and to cherish goodness, love, patience, joy and peace. She can be stubborn in her witness to these aspirations, and she can repent and regret her own failings as she comes to recognise them. In this sense Elizabeth Bennett is shown in the story to be the real priest, the one who continues to trust in the triumph of goodness over adversity, of true love over human failings and wickedness. Her faith and her persistence give her particular 'ministry' the attributes of priestliness: helping others to recognise and accept the grace of God to connect their own vocations and ministries with the structures of salvation in this human life. Her trust and persistence in the high aspirations of that society, amidst the living community which valued these things in a mixed way, allowed some of the characters to find fulfilment and a sense of direction.

Here is a fascinating model of a very mixed range of vocations and ministries being explored at many levels of selfishness, and of the search for salvation. Within this maelstrom one person can be seen to exercise a priestly ministry, based not on her own perfections but on her trust and patience in the victory of love over all that is less than love. The key place for this ministry and priesthood to be worked out is in the context of the view that 'the thing to work on is three or four families in a country village'.

This says something important about the scale and scope and nature of ministry and priesthood for most of the baptised: the appropriate exercise of the priesthood of all believers. Amidst the complexities, the successes and the setbacks of the exploration of vocation and ministry, there will be occasions when particular people can make a specific contribution to the more self-conscious connecting with the grace of God as relationships and aspirations are renewed and restored and structures of salvation clarified.

Elizabeth Bennett and priestly ministry

If we consider Elizabeth Bennett as exercising a priestly ministry in this story, we should note eight main features. First, the effectiveness of her helping the cause of salvation is much more profound than that of the institutional church and her appointed priests. Nonetheless there was an important public role for the church and its clergy. Elizabeth was formed and nourished in this context. What might this tell us about the relationship of the 'priesthood of all believers' to the institutional church?

Second, Elizabeth believed in universal verities but was concerned with them in a very small and immediate circle. Is there something important about the scale and scope of such ministry if it is to be 'priestly'?

Third, Elizabeth suffered from pride and prejudice as much as the other characters. She remained faithful to the cause of love and was willing to see new things and make fresh judgements. What might this tell us about spirituality and priestly ministry?

Fourth, much of Elizabeth's 'ministry' (in the sense of serving others and contributing to the unfolding of vocations) was not directly priestly. Is there an important distinction between pastoral ministry and priesthood?

Fifth, despite her failings, her faithfulness enabled her to hold on to these high aspirations for others too. In a sense she sometimes acted as a vicar, a vicarious one, holding the faith for others when they were distressed or hurt or otherwise occupied. Does this say something about pastoral ministry which might become priesthood?

Sixth, what Elizabeth stands for is not her own agenda but that of the Christian society in which she is set. The priesthood of all believers comes from the grace of baptism and commitment to the story and the resources already given to the church. How best can our own 'vocation and ministry' be rooted in this story and these resources?

Seventh, it could be argued that the novel describes in detail Elizabeth's ministry, and that this becomes 'priestly' at particular moments and for particular occasions. Is this a realistic understanding of ministry and priesthood and their interrelationship, or a misleading one?

Eighth, the tension between the highest aspirations and human failings is worked out in the local community, serviced by the priestly ministry of Elizabeth Bennett. There is no mention of the place of public worship or of private prayer. How would you relate these activities to an understanding of ministry and priesthood? Is worship the place where:

- the 'highest aspirations' are focused;
- the 'mix' of human beings is recognised;
- the key people who are called to relate these two things are nourished and guided?

EXERCISE
📖 **Read John 4:1–42.**

Make notes of your reflections about pastoral and priestly ministry in this story as seen in:
- Jesus;
- the Samaritan woman.

If we consider this story from the point of view of the Samaritan woman discovering something of her vocation to a particular ministry we can note the following twelve points:

1. Initially she does not ask anything of Jesus; he asks something of her. Ministry may not be about pursuing our own concerns even to receive good things from Jesus: it may be rooted in learning to

perceive his needs in the place where he meets us. He needs us to minister to him.

2. The Samaritan woman has no proper qualifications in terms of theological understanding or devotional discipline. Despite the tendency in the modern church to link all notions of ministering with the need for training, the Samaritan woman has had no proper training!

3. The life story of the Samaritan woman has been an unsuccessful search for fulfilment. She has had five husbands and now a live-in lover. She too has a need, though it is not yet clearly recognised. She will require this degree of self-awareness if she is to minister to others.

4. Despite her intellectual and moral failings, the Samaritan woman can fulfil the law. She can love her enemy. She is willing to consider giving a drink to a Jew. The key is not his apparent status or viewpoint, but his need. Her recognition of this fact qualifies her to be a minister, a servant of the needs of Jesus and his gospel. She can be a vehicle of his living water because she is willing to be generous to a person in human need. Thus she fulfils the law and the commandment to love because she has a generous heart, the life of God within her.

5. The Samaritan woman knows how to work the well, thus she is already familiar with the rhythm of need and the response which is necessary to meet it. Now she has to learn that this is how God works in us and with us.

6. The Samaritan woman is honest about her own shortcomings.

7. The Samaritan woman is not concerned about her own need in this encounter (symbolised by her bucket which needs filling). She is concerned about worship and truth. These are the two areas in which Jesus is truly met and ministry clearly focused. Each places us in a larger context.

8. The key to worship and truth is the Messiah.

9. When the Samaritan woman meets the Messiah and hears the words 'I am he', she asks for no further clarification or assistance with her own journey: immediately she becomes a missionary and goes off to bear witness to others in her town, to build bridges between her experience of knowing something of God's grace and the needs of other people. Her 'ministry' among her people becomes priestly, symbolised no longer by the bucket but by the words of her witness. From this moment she becomes a priest to her

people. No doubt she continued to draw water for human need, but on this occasion she became more self-consciously the agent of living water.

10. Some people in her community respond to the witness of the Samaritan woman and come to the Messiah themselves. When they meet him, he becomes the focus and fount of their faith; they have no need for the priestly ministry of the woman. Her ministry at the well continues but her priestly role has passed. It was crucial – for a moment.

11. The woman who brought life to others with her bucket can be an agent of living water, eternity. Her exercise of priesthood is rooted in the kind of person she is anyway, not in some special or radically different role. There is an important continuity of vocation which embraces our ministry and its potential for priesthood.

12. For this Samaritan woman the exercise of priestly ministry involves meeting the Messiah with a generous heart, recognising his needs and going back to her community to help give birth to his new life in its midst. That is a powerful image of priestly ministry which occurs frequently in the biblical narrative.

EXERCISE
📖 **Re-read John 4:1–42.**

How does this narrative shape your views on ministry?

What do you think?

Here are some features of the passage for consideration:

1. The woman discovered the occasion and direction of call, not through interpreting her own life experience, nor through the tradition (Jacob's well), but through generosity of heart in the face of apparently human need. What does this say about the call to ministry, particularly to priestly ministry?

2. Like Elizabeth Bennett, the Samaritan woman had a limited, local role. She was called to be a particular focus and then to retire. Is there something 'occasional' and 'momentary' about pastoral ministry which becomes priestly?

3. Faith in the Messiah is crucial to recognising and receiving living

water, for the woman and for her community. Is our understanding of pastoral ministry too concerned with 'caring' and not clear enough about the centrality of the Messiah?

4. The symbol of the bucket and the image of living water point to a basic continuity in the development of the woman's vocation. How can we be open to 'new life', yet honour what God has already given us?

Further reading

Austen, J (1972), *Pride and Prejudice*, Harmondsworth, Penguin.

Barry, F R (1958), *Vocation and Ministry*, London, Hodder and Stoughton.

Eccelstone, G (ed.) (1988), *The Parish Church*, London, Mowbray.

Green, L (1987), *Power to the Powerless*, London, Marshall Morgan and Scott.

Guiver, G (1988), *Company of Voices: daily prayer and the people of God*, London, SPCK.

Hauerwas, S (1981), *A Community of Character: toward a constructive Christian social ethic*, Notre Dame, Indiana, University of Notre Dame Press.

Kraemer, H (1958), *A Theology of the Laity*, London, Lutterworth.

Sheils, W and Wood, D (eds) (1989), *The Ministry: clerical and lay (Studies in Church History no. 26)*, Oxford, Blackwell.

Vanstone, W H (1977), *Love's Endeavour, Love's Expense*, London, Darton, Longman and Todd.

3. PUBLIC MINISTRY: THE IMPORTANCE OF DISTANCE

Introduction

We have seen that in the unfolding vocation of each Christian there is a developing pattern of ministry: formal and informal, conscious and subconscious, appropriate and inappropriate, grace-bearing and sinful. Sometimes this ministerial activity crystallises into something more overtly priestly, though each of the baptised is commissioned to be resolute in faith so that their actions and intentions can be best used in the service of the gospel and the coming of the Kingdom.

In short, the priesthood of all believers issues in ministerial activity which can be grace-bearing, yet on occasion this will be more overtly 'priestly' in its focus and performance. The aim of all Christian ministers is to enhance the priestly mediating of grace through our discipleship.

However, there has always been a role for a more formally constituted priesthood within the overall ministry of the Christian church. In the next chapter we shall examine the history of formal priesthood and leadership, but first it is important to try to identify some of the distinguishing features of public as opposed to purely personal ministry.

Reflecting on experience

Look at your answers to questions 4, 5, 6 and 7 of the Ministry Questionnaire which you completed as part of the work for chapter 1. Then consider the following questions:

Identify the different forms of public ministry in your local church. What are the reasons for the differences? How are these different forms connected to each other? How do they relate to any notion of vocation for the individual and for the church?

▶▶

How are people in public ministry perceived by members of the church and by people in the wider community?

Do those in public ministry possess any kind of authority? If so, where does it come from, how is it limited and reviewed, and how is it accountable?

How does the exercise of public ministry relate to public worship?

A day in the life of the vicar: a case study

Richard was feeling under pressure. He had been the vicar of St Mary's for three years now and the honeymoon was over. He had enjoyed his curacy in a large well-attended suburban church and his first living on a working-class estate on the edge of a major town, but now at St Mary's the pressures were different. It was the parish church of a town of some 15,000 people, and although he had the help of a curate, a reader, and a retired priest, most people still wanted 'the vicar' when anything needed to be done.

His diary for that day, a Thursday, revealed some of the problems. It read:

0800	Morning Prayer
0900	school assembly
1000	funeral of Mrs Baker
1100	Holy Communion
1200	meet with headmaster re school governors' meeting
1300	Rotary lunch
	hospital visiting
1600	school governors' meeting
1815	re-marriage case
1930	church council

Morning Prayer was said with the curate, the reader and a couple of lay people who usually attended. Richard found that half-hour an essential start to the day, partly for the sake of his own relationship with God but also because he had always believed that praying for the parish was one of the more important things the church offered the community. In his own mind at least, he followed the advice of his training vicar and 'laid his diary on the altar'. Spiritually that helped, but it did not solve the practical pressures. Indeed it was practical pressures that had led him to agree with the others that Evensong would be said privately: there never seemed to be a time when they could all be there together.

Richard usually tried to go to school assembly at the local church primary school each Thursday whether he was taking it or not. It only took half an hour and he thought it was important to be seen regularly by the children; certainly the staff appreciated his interest and involvement.

Mrs Baker was one of the stalwarts of St Mary's and her funeral in the church was well attended. Fortunately the crematorium was in the town so it was possible to take the committal there and get back for the regular Thursday morning communion. This was a *Book of Common Prayer* service attended by about a dozen people, mainly retired. It was normally taken by the retired priest but he had phoned to say that he was 'under the weather'. The curate was away on a post-ordination training day so there was only Richard. He liked to take it occasionally as it kept him in touch with that group, but he wished it was not necessary that day.

The school governors' meeting was of a local secondary school. Richard had been invited to become a governor when he was appointed to St Mary's. 'We've always had the vicar with us', was how it was put to him, and he valued the contact it gave him with pupils and their parents, many of whom had few other connections with the church. The trouble was that it soon became clear that there were various factions on the governing body, and as Richard was considered neutral he was not entirely surprised when one day the headmaster privately begged him to allow his name to go forward as chairman. Somewhat reluctantly Richard agreed. Certainly it gave him a high profile in the local community, but it also added dramatically to the workload. The extra meeting with the headmaster was typical but the head, quite rightly, wanted to fill Richard in on the background to an item on the agenda that afternoon.

Jane, Richard's wife, was pretty fed up about his disappearing off to the Rotary lunch each Thursday. 'We have little enough time together as it is', she said. But he had been invited to join soon after he had arrived in the parish and apart from the fact that it was another good way into the community, he enjoyed the company of some of the others in the club. It was also a good lunch!

After lunch he called at home. There were messages from undertakers asking for him to take funerals the following week, and among the letters was one from the bishop asking him to serve on a diocesan working party to look at the diocese's response to the Decade of Evangelism. Richard had once remarked at a deanery discussion that he shared Archbishop Runcie's opinion that 'It was the genius of the Church of England to cast evangelism in the context of pastoral care'. Somehow this had got back to the bishop and now he wanted Richard to serve on the group in order to represent that point of view. Richard knew that others on the group wanted a diocesan initiative which would take a far more openly evangelistic stance towards the community, and he feared that could create a suspicion of the church which might lessen the opportunities for community service which he had tried to build up. To serve would be to attend an endless series of meetings which probably would not produce a common mind at the end, but to refuse to serve would be a 'cop-out'. He was not sure what to do.

There were usually a few people in the local hospital whom he knew. The regular ward visiting was done by a neighbouring parish priest, who was also a part-time chaplain, but Richard liked to visit at least once a week to see those who would expect him to come. He also knew a number of the staff and normally bumped into one or other of them on his weekly visits. They seemed to value seeing him around.

The school governors' meeting was fraught. It was not helped by Richard getting there a minute or so late. A parishioner in the hospital wanted to talk and Richard felt bad about having to leave, but no one at the meeting would appreciate his dilemma since they had a long agenda. Fortunately they had agreed to a proposal that no meetings should last longer than two hours. There was a problem with a member of staff, the subject of Richard's earlier meeting with the headmaster, and Richard knew that resolving it would not be easy. He was right. There was also the on-going saga of the battle with the local education authority about the placing of a unit for those with special educational needs. Mrs Jones, the parent governor with an axe to grind on that issue, took some handling, as did the county councillor governor who always felt he had to defend the authority's decisions.

Richard's predecessor had introduced the practice of selectively re-marrying divorced people and he had done so with at least the tacit approval of the bishop. Richard was happy to continue the practice and certainly the community now expected the parish church to do this, although it was widely recognised that it was not automatic and cases had to be investigated. This always entailed meeting the couple and going into the circumstances of the previous marriage. Richard sometimes wondered whether those who thought that clergy led protected lives had any idea of the things he had read about in some couples' divorce papers.

He arrived back at the vicarage just as the couple appeared. David, Richard's twelve-year-old son, asked Richard to give him some help with a difficult bit of his homework and Richard said he would try to help him before the church council meeting. The couple's case turned out to be particularly complicated and by the time they had finished Richard had to go straight to the church council. He apologised to David and said he was sure Jane could help him. Jane gave him one of her long-suffering looks.

The church council had the usual rag-bag of items, some more contentious than others. Over the past two and a half years the church had managed to raise money to re-order the choir vestry, which was very unsatisfactory for the choir. However, an outbreak of dry rot in the church hall had been a nasty surprise and some members of the church council wanted to spend the money raised on dealing with that first. The choirmaster was not impressed and a member of the choir who was on the church council could be guaranteed to put his point of view forward forcibly. Some wanted rather to cut the parish's giving to overseas missions, and that caused a row. Referring it back to the finance committee only put off the day of decision.

Richard also presented to the church council a paper on establishing and training a group of lay visitors. His predecessor had done a good job in involving lay people in church services, reading lessons, taking intercessions and so on, but it had evidently proved very difficult to get much co-ordinated lay involvement in the church's pastoral ministry. Among the congregation there was a lot of simple 'good neighbourliness', but little desire to do anything openly on behalf of the church. 'People expect the vicar' is what Richard was often told, and he had more than a suspicion that behind that remark was an implied criticism of his community involvement. 'Some of them just want a private chaplain and resent any wider role', was how he put it to the archdeacon at his ministerial review meeting. Richard was grateful that at least the archdeacon supported a larger vision of the parish priest's task. The paper was accepted, but without much enthusiasm. Implementing it, Richard knew, would be difficult.

The argument about money and lay visiting went on longer than he anticipated and he was half an hour late for supper. Jane understood, it had happened so often before.

That night Richard lay awake for some time. Two things worried him. First, there was the problem of Michael, the Reader. He was an able and intelligent man who had retired from a university lecturing post and who wanted to give more time to the church. Academically he had no problems with the Readers' course and soon qualified. His sermons were well constructed, thoughtful and theologically very well-informed. Richard always enjoyed listening to him and found him an intellectually stimulating colleague. However, some in the congregation were always complaining that what he said went over their heads, and this was not helped by Michael's occasional sharp tongue. He could appear to those who were alarmed by his academic background as aloof and even arrogant. 'I wonder whether some of them have got any heads to go over', he remarked to Richard once. The problem had become acute with the warden of a home for the elderly people in the parish. Michael had said he wanted to do some work with the elderly and Richard had asked him to visit this home and take a fortnightly service. Now the warden had told Richard that they would prefer the retired priest to come, as the residents found him more sympathetic. The retired priest had agreed without realising the background, and was embarrassed when Richard explained the situation. But the harm was done. Explaining that to Michael was not going to be easy.

Then also at the back of Richard's mind was a remark by Paul Ivors, the managing director of the main firm in the town, whom Richard had met at the mayor's reception the evening before. Ivors was not a churchman and Richard had never had the opportunity of meeting him before, but over drinks in the mayor's parlour he had told Richard how much he liked the medieval architecture of St Mary's and how he always included it on his itinerary with guests when they were visiting town. They had got on well in their brief conversation and it had ended with Ivors' suggestion that Richard should come to visit his factory some time. Richard said he would, but he wondered what the workforce would make of his visit. Some in his congregation worked for the firm and Ivors had the reputation of being a fair but very tough businessman who did not shirk from making people redundant when costs had to be cut. One member of the congregation was particularly offended by the manner of his dismissal. As Richard drifted off into sleep he wondered where it would all lead.

EXERCISE

What are the main pressures facing Richard? Who is making demands? What is being demanded?

What are the expectations of Richard:

* in terms of ministry;
* in terms of leadership;
* in terms of theological expertise;
* in terms of family life;
* in terms of the local church?

Reflections on Richard's day

The author of this story about 'Richard' was the Venerable Bob Reiss, Archdeacon of Surrey. He offers the following reflection upon Richard's day, considering in turn the perspectives of the family, the congregation, the people on the fringes of the church, the institutions with which Richard interacts, and Richard's own perspective and rationale.

Family

At an ordination the bishop asks those to be ordained, 'Will you strive to fashion your life and that of your household according to the way of Christ?' Jane could have been forgiven for thinking that might mean a little more than saying goodbye to her husband at 7.45a.m. and only seeing him as he rushed through the family home until nearly 10.00p.m. at night when they finally sat down for an all-too-late supper. David, their son, had even more cause for complaint. Clergy are expected to be exemplary as partners and parents, and yet their job invades their home and their privacy more than in many other professions, and the family can feel the strain. Any sensitive parish priest will feel the tension between his or her responsibilities to the family and the demands of the ministerial role. We can hope that Richard made time for his family at other times during the week, but the priest who dismisses a real emergency 'because it is my day off' will not escape criticism.

Congregation

Congregations expect their vicar to conduct worship in the way they want and to preach intelligible sermons; but as the example showed, a congregation, particularly a large town centre one, will contain a number of varied and conflicting expectations both about the style of worship and about the type of sermons that will be considered appropriate. As in other areas of life you cannot please everyone all the time.

The congregation will also expect the vicar to provide guidance and even leadership in the decisions that any church has to take. There was a spiritual dimension to the priorities in spending that Richard and the church council had to face, and Richard remembered that at ordination the bishop had told him he was to be a 'messenger, watchman and steward of the Lord' and he had 'to teach and admonish, to feed and provide for the Lord's family, to search for his children in the wilderness of this world's temptations and to guide them through its confusions'. However, he had also promised 'to promote unity, peace and love among all Christian people'. Getting that right in the context of a divided church council is not always easy.

Then congregations also expect to be visited regularly, probably far more frequently than is practicable, and want their priest to be a companion and spiritual guide in their sorrow and joy. Much of that the priest will find a privilege and pleasure. It would be the very unlucky minister who could find no friends among his congregation, but the demands can be taxing and the criticism swift if expectations are not met. A hint of that was there in the reaction to Richard's plans for a training course for lay visitors.

Fringe

Beyond the congregation there is that large body of people known sometimes as 'the fringe'. Many who rarely, if ever, attend the parish church still feel it is theirs and believe they have some claim on the vicar's time and attention. Often that will not be disputed; the warden of the elderly people's home could reasonably expect some pastoral care from the church for those housebound in the home, while the undertaker's search for a Church of England minister to take funerals only reflected what the bereaved will have wanted. Pastoral care of the sick, bereaved, housebound and disadvantaged is implicit in the charge of the ordinal if it is accepted that 'God's children' does not simply mean those who go to church. Many members of the church will expect their vicar to be involved in that way. However, ministry rarely leads to enlarged congregations. Still less does it generate significant income for the parish church. Financial stringency and a culture that can sometimes demand visible measures of 'success' can subtly undermine a ministry that sees the task as responding with Christian love to all in the parish without any desire for obvious reward.

Institutions

Beyond the demands of individuals, there are also institutions that can lay claims on the vicar. Some, like Richard's church school, uniformed organisations and the Mother's Union, may be officially sponsored by the church and the vicar will be expected to be involved in their lives. Few would deny that he should know and be known by them.

Others, like the hospital in Richard's parish, some educational institutions or a military barracks looking for a local priest as an officiating chaplain, are prepared to pay for a chaplaincy role. Most large organisations from time to time have to deal with personal crises like a sudden injury, an unexpected bereavement or, increasingly, redundancy. They recognise that a chaplain, with a loyalty to something beyond the institution and with no personal status to uphold, can bring a dimension to caring for the individual that it is very difficult for others within the organisation to provide. Some industrial chaplains have found that those made redundant respond to them more positively than to the personnel officer, no matter how caring and genuine that officer may be, because the officer is still an employee of the company.

The fact that chaplains stand outside the institution and have that other loyalty also gives them a freedom that is often valued. An example from the author's contribution to *Say One for Me* (Carr, 1992, p. 22) makes the point.

> When the newspapers were full of allegations of bullying and brutality in the army, one senior officer said that he and other senior officers thought that the chaplain's presence and independence, as well as the army's respect for the chaplain's confidentiality and his right of direct access to the commanding officer, gave him a significant role in dealing with something about which they were all extremely concerned but uncertain how to respond. They acknowledged the need for ministry.

Some school chaplains can tell a similar story.

Other institutions, like school governing bodies or voluntary social work organisations, have no funds to offer but they still value the contribution that the church can make to their deliberations. Richard's secondary school 'likes to have the vicar here' because he represents the community beyond the school. Such bodies feel a need to be accountable, and the vicar is a useful ally. They may sense that the vicar has a range of contacts through the community which could be useful for their institution, and they may even feel that he or she can harness such influence as the church can bring on local political decisions. Where the church is respected, and provided the effect is not weakened by too frequent use, a well-argued public statement from the church in a newspaper can still have some effect.

Richard's rationale

Just being the vicar is no guarantee of being respected. Richard had to prove his impartiality and competence before he was asked to become chairman of the governors, just as he had to relate easily to Paul Ivors before he was invited to the factory. The challenge of having to establish trust and prove competence in outwardly secular institutions may put some clergy off being involved in the first place, and certainly 'playing away from home' is more difficult. Richard's work with the church council was taxing enough, but at least he knew the language and after a few years in ministry had learnt most of the rules. At the school, and even more in Paul Ivors' factory, he felt he was in mysterious territory. The internal machinations of the local educational authority and the pressures of the market had not been on the syllabus at his theological college. At times he could feel exposed.

But there were also other, more subtle temptations. As chairman of governors it was possible to get totally absorbed by the issues and to think that this was the 'real world' compared with the often relatively petty concerns that dominated the church council. Certainly the sums of money involved at the school were far larger. There were times when Richard was tempted to treat the church almost as irrelevant.

What prevented him from succumbing to that was Morning Prayer. When he 'laid his diary on the altar' he brought the concerns of the governors' meeting to God in prayer and he realised it was that which made his schoolwork into a ministry. Without the discipline of prayer he would simply have been another well-meaning, public-spirited citizen. Praying did not give him instantaneous answers, it was not a mechanism into some secret revelation, but praying meant that he brought the school to God and God to the school. And Richard came to believe that was the essence of ministry.

Richard's theology

It all came to the fore in discussion at the diocesan working party on which Richard eventually agreed to serve. One of the members argued for an evangelistic campaign throughout the diocese that would involve the distribution of tracts and invitations to public meetings in the cathedral and other major churches, including St Mary's. Richard wondered aloud what effect that might have on the church's pastoral work, and he was challenged to defend his emphasis on pastoral involvement with the community. 'Where does it lead?' he was asked. 'How many more people have been brought to Christ through this work? How is the congregation encouraged by it?'

Richard's response to these questions was firmly rooted in a doctrine of creation as he argued his case in the following terms.

> God saw all that he had made, and it was very good. I know sin has disrupted that original goodness but I do not believe that it has completely obliterated it. The world that I am involved in, the whole world of the community including its institutions, is, I believe, of God. And if God be God then my responsibility is not to imagine I am taking God to the community, but to find him there. Sometimes, when the opportunity is right, I can then point him out to others, but it is not because I possess God as a gift to give. He is the gift which sometimes I find. My task is then to interpret what has happened so that others can see him as well.
>
> And what I find is that God is present, not just through the goodness of creation but through redemption as well. God's way of working was focused in Christ, and he continues to work in that way. So when I see good coming out of evil, love transforming bitterness, forgiveness healing injury, I believe that is of God.
>
> Occasionally I can serve that process. I never know in advance how it is going to happen. The situations are often messy and ambiguous, but by praying and by trying to love, I can sometimes be an instrument of God's peace. I do not think it is fanciful to relate that to the incarnation and the cross. Of course my struggle is nothing like as awful as Christ's, but it is a struggle to love, and through that to make sense of things and to interpret them.
>
> I do not know how many people glimpse something of God through my attempts to interpret what happens. When I am invited to some secular organisation I am not quite sure what they want, but they know I am a priest, a 'walking sacrament' as Austin Farrer

once put it. They know that in some way I stand for God and his presence in the world, and I suppose in some curious way my being there shows that God is there as well. T S Eliot once talked about 'the still point in the turning world'. Well, maybe that is what I point to by being in the place, and that might just make some people there reflect on the values and purposes of the institution as part of God's world.

I have no idea whether that brought any of them to church more regularly or even at all. Each Sunday there is a regular core, but then there are a lot of others who come less frequently and they are not the same people each week. Overall the numbers remain fairly steady, and as some are going through death or moving away I suppose others must be coming to replace them. I hope through worship and preaching, some in the congregation catch something of the Christian vision of God in the world and begin to see themselves as ministers as well. When they come to church they may be there by themselves, but in their hearts and minds they bring their families, their friends, their concerns. I hope our worship helps them to interpret their experience and to see God in it all, and maybe in their way they help others to see that as well.

That may not encourage them in the way that a huge increase in numbers and money might encourage them, but the experience of Christ in Gethsemane and on Calvary tells me that God does not work through the big battalions. Helping people at St Mary's to see themselves as sharing in Christian ministry by recognising and pointing to God at work in the world, including in their lives, and doing that myself in some way for the community, is what I think evangelism is all about.

And my involvement with the community is not some additional bit of work after I have done the basic Christian ministry to the congregation. Involvement in God's world is the basic Christian ministry. I belong on the edge of the church's life as its representative to the community, and if I allow myself to get totally sucked into the church's life then I have abandoned the Church of England's ministry and become purely sectarian.

Richard's response did not persuade all of the working party, and as he feared they could not present a unanimous report. Some churches in the diocese went ahead with the campaign with tracts and big events and it brought some new people into those churches. Whether it damaged their relationship with the rest of the community was, Richard thought, for others to judge.

But it did not happen at St Mary's, and there is still that gentle drifting in and out of people from the congregation.

EXERCISE
How do Bob Reiss's reflections compare with your own?

'I belong on the edge of the church's life as its representative to the community.' Is this the best way to describe public ministry? What are the advantages and disadvantages of this way of thinking?

Beginning ministry

Many churches have a special service to induct people into public ministry. For some forms of public ministry it is an ordination; for other forms of public ministry it may be a service of licensing or commissioning.

EXERCISE
Obtain a copy of a service of ordination, licensing or commissioning. Read it through and make notes of the features that point to what is *distinctive* about public ministry.

Some of these distinctive features will be:
- special authorisation by representative figure(s) from the wider church community;
- Bible readings about call and commissioning;
- a description of the role for which the candidate is to be given public authorisation;
- confirmation that the candidate has been properly prepared and examined for this work;
- an emphasis upon the essential complementarity between this particular ministry and those of other members of the body of Christ;
- a public 'presentation' of the candidate to be approved and received in their new role by the church and community;

- a testing of the candidate's own sense of call (vocation) and fitness for this role or office in the church: often by posing questions about personal discipline and loyalty to the doctrines and practices of the church;
- prayers which invoke the blessing of the Holy Spirit on those to be public ministers;
- prayers of all those present: for the public minister, for the church, for the mission of the gospel, for the world, and for themselves and their own vocation and ministry;
- presentation to the candidate of a Bible, and perhaps other items, as symbol of both the authority received and the resources to be used.

EXERCISE
From your analysis of liturgies for commissioning public ministry, what would you highlight as the chief characteristics, from the point of view of:
- the candidate;
- the sponsoring church;
- the worshipping church;
- the wider community?

EXERCISE
📖 **Read 2 Kings 4:8–37.**

Make notes about Elisha as a public minister.

If we consider the story in 2 Kings 4:8–37 as an illustration of Elisha exercising a public ministry in a way which enabled the Shunammite woman to receive something profound in terms of God's grace and new life, then we can note the following eight points:

1. She accepts Elisha as a 'man of God', that is, she recognises that God calls and commissions some people to a public, authoritative ministry which brings his presence and power more clearly into people's lives.
2. She makes a separate chamber for the 'holy man'. She wants to be in relation to this person of God yet knows that he stands for

something which is part of, yet beyond, the normal confines of her domestic life.

3. Although she is a rich woman she does not seek parity or friendship. She recognises the need for a proper distance between herself and this holy person. Thus she does not invite him to sit at her table, she provides a separate and special space. It is this difference in space and perspective which allows her to receive something of God through him. Their intercourse is not simply human: there is special provision for the divine. This is enacted by the fact that she stands in the doorway: on the edge of this space is the place priest and people meet, hence all the various courtyards in the Temple.

4. Because Elisha stands for some kind of otherness, the woman can trust to him her deepest desire, her desire for a son. Our true vocation is something about the birth of God's life in us.

5. There is an enormous setback. The birth of her son is eventually followed by his death. What God has given has been mysteriously taken away. Often in scripture all that is precious in God's gift is taken away and destroyed. Like Job, we are constantly challenged to know our total dependence upon the mysterious grace of God.

6. The woman goes to Elisha muttering the refrain 'all will be well'. She has lain her dead vocation in the holy place. She refuses to deal with Elisha's assistant for only the duly appointed holy person can help. It mirrors our own tendency to say that 'only a visit from the vicar will do'. She needs resources from beyond the normal human environment of kindness and concern.

7. The holy man comes to the special place, and with prayer and laying on of hands the child is restored to life. God's true life comes through death and resurrection: a letting go of humanness to receive back the miracle of divine life. This miracle is pure gift. We cannot earn it or own it; we can only receive such new life through the ministry of those called and commissioned to stand apart and meet us on the boundary between humanness and holiness.

8. Elisha was the agent of her receiving new life, not through skilled pastoral practice (he hardly speaks to her) but through helping her to trust that 'all will be well' and to seek grace in the special space and through the special person raised up by God for this purpose.

EXERCISE
📖 Re-read 2 Kings 4:8–37.

Compare the forms of public ministry exercised by Elisha and Richard.

What do you think?

Here are some further issues for consideration:

1. Compare and contrast the roles of Elisha and Richard as public ministers in regard to:
   - sense of authority;
   - use of space;
   - pastoral practice;
   - use of prayer, liturgy, ritual;
   - relationships to others.
2. What is the importance of 'distance' between public minister and private person?
3. To what extent should a public minister be a set-apart person, using set-apart texts (scripture, creeds) and set-apart places?
4. How do your reflections about the practice of public ministry relate to the liturgies used to commission it?
5. What is the proper relationship of the centre and periphery in church life?

Further reading

Carroll, J W (1996), *As One With Authority*, Philadelphia, Pennsylvania, Westminster Press.

Carr, W (1985), *The Priestlike Task: a model for developing and training the church's ministry*, London, SPCK.

Carr, W (1992), *Say One For Me*, London, SPCK.

Moody, C (1992), *Eccentric Ministry*, London, Darton, Longman and Todd.

Ramsey, M (1985), *The Christian Priest Today*, London, SPCK.

Schillebeeckx, E (1985), *The Church with a Human Face*, London, SCM.

4. PUBLIC MINISTRY: HISTORY AND DOCTRINE

Introduction

We have considered some of the characteristics of public ministry. We have seen that it is focused in someone who is especially called, prepared, commissioned and received as a leader and holy person; it operates on the boundary between divinity and humanity, representing something of God to humankind and something of humankind to God.

In this chapter we shall examine the development of doctrines of ministry, with particular reference to priesthood and public representative ministries. We begin with two images of public ministry.

Reflecting on experience
Think of a non-church group or organisation to which you belong, or of which you have some knowledge:
- to what extent does it have certain designated people to perform particular roles?
- what are the advantages and disadvantages of this way of working?
- how, and for what reasons, are people appointed to various roles?
- should this way of working apply to the church, or does God require something different?

The sheepdog

Sue Walrond-Skinner provides the following image of public ministry, based on the sheepdog. She is an ordained minister who works as Adviser in Pastoral Care and Counselling in the Southwark Diocese.

Years of watching and working with border collies suggests to me the fruitfulness of the shepherd dog as a model for the ordained ministry. Others have seen the potential in this image before, so I claim nothing new. For me it begins from a natural association with the pastoral task of ministry, with the Good Shepherd and those fundamental though somewhat ambivalent metaphors that undergird much of our pastoral theology.

The sheepdog possesses two all-consuming attractions: the sheep and her master. Her eye stays focused always on the sheep; her ear listens ceaselessly for the shepherd's call. Her attractions to both are profound, fundamentally part of her nature; neither has to be learnt. Yet neither attraction can be worked out for her without the contrary pull of the other. She is held into a triangular relationship with shepherd and sheep; her wild, compulsive instincts are only kept in check by her unswerving attention to her master.

Yet these instincts are the very energy which fuels her attraction to the sheep. Her attentiveness is driven by all that is wild within her, all those untamed forces of energy that compel her to control, to attack and subdue her prey. And it is precisely *because* these instincts are so well developed in her that the border collie sheepdog is *the* choice of helpmate for the shepherd.

However, the paradox of her excellence lies in the juxtaposition of this untamed energy with her parallel delight in her relationship with her master. Obedient but never servile, the border collie's relationship with the shepherd holds in tension her pull towards the sheep and her even stronger compulsion to become part of the shepherd's own purposes, so closely a part that she seems at times to be simply an extension of his own will. But this is always an illusion. The grace and beauty and fulfilment of all that constitutes the 'isness' of the dog resides in the way she dissolves herself completely into the shepherd's will and yet goes on experiencing the strength of her own instincts.

Sheepdogs lie about a lot. They are capable of putting every fibre of their being to work when required to do so, but they are instantly at ease, able to leave the sheep to get on with their lives, feeding, communicating, just 'being' together. The sheepdog does not interfere or interrupt the life and work of the flock. The sheep are always the focus, the dog is merely an instrument which exists for their welfare and a tool that is usable by the shepherd in his own care of them.

The dog does not enact her own will with regard to the sheep; she enables the shepherd to enact *his* will for them. She must allow her own wilfulness to be overcome in obedience to the master. She is focused beyond herself and finds perfect fulfilment in accomplishing her master's will, and she expects and receives his reward.

Interaction between the centre and the edge

Joe Hasler provides a contrasting image of public ministry. He is an ordained minister who works as incumbent of an urban priority area parish.

Before I was in ordained ministry I was employed as a community development worker. In this job I was employed to intervene in other people's situations in ways where they were left to take the initiative and make the decisions. I remember one woman describing my role as 'the pole at the back rather than the pole in the middle'.

By virtue of being on the margins I could provide an enabling role, a non-directive ministry, that enabled the groups to gain confidence and power. It involved helping the distribution of resources and improving the relationships between different groups of people.

I could gladly see this role as a diaconal one. It resonates with the appointment of Stephen and the seven in Acts. They were appointed in a situation where the distribution of food and the settling of discontent between the Jews and the Greeks was paramount.

Since I have been ordained as a priest, the eucharistic role places me centrally, behind the altar, as the president. This role includes receiving the bread offered, bread that represents so many different people offering themselves. Along with the bread is offered the tensions between these varying selves. I have become profoundly aware that what I do is the very act that makes for a focus of unity. I am now a central 'actor'.

Being central as the president does not mean I have abandoned operating from the margins. On the one hand, when I preside I am central. But I can also list a number of other times when I am marginal. From the pulpit I can be a 'commentator' verging on prophet. At the church council I can be a 'ring holder' for the debate. When I am counselling I can stand as an 'outsider'. When I am peacekeeping I can create pathways between groups of people so they can learn each other's language. On many occasions I stand firmly on, or across, the boundaries.

It is not too easy to describe this model, when in the eyes of many people I am oscillating from the centre to the edge. But I am sure people do sense that I not only travel from the edge to the middle and back again, but that I take stuff with me. This is probably most evident by the way I am heard to pray.

If I were pressed to find an image for this oscillation I would probably get all organic and talk about lungs breathing or hearts beating. However, it is definitely a process image that involves the interaction between the centre and the edges as its driving energy.

EXERCISE

Comment on these two images, especially in relation to the idea that 'sheepdogs lie about a lot' and of 'travelling from the edge to the middle and back again'.

Development of authorised public ministry

Most scholars agree that the New Testament does not give clear guidelines about patterns and styles of ministry. Jesus is seen and interpreted in a variety of ways: prophet, priest, king, shepherd, servant and healer, among many others. Paul's famous image of the body shows that members of the church have a great variety of gifts and contributions, all of which have a proper place, under the one headship of Christ. The New Testament indicates that the whole people of God share in a priestly ministry which is exercised in a number of ways according to the needs and gifts of communities and individuals. There is mention of different roles and functions, including deacons, widows, presbyters (elders), bishops, apostles, evangelists, teachers and prophets.

As the early church increased in size and complexity, and as it had to define the gospel more clearly over against Jewish, Greek and other cultures, so there was an increasing need for a more defined shape in terms of organisation, officers and authority. As a result the order of bishop, and then of priest or presbyter, developed to be a focus for unity and authenticity. These roles were especially expressed in the celebration of the eucharist, which was recognised as a community action but requiring its unity and authenticity to be represented in those commissioned to continue the apostles' work as 'the spiritual leaders' of the primitive churches.

Paul recognised the unique calling of the first apostles and of a proper division of territorial responsibilities between them. The primary function of an apostle was the preaching of the gospel, the establishing of churches and their continuing supervision. Yet in his own ministry as an apostle, Paul clearly recognised the integrity of local churches and the fact that apostles are servants of the church, not its masters. Initially there was an organic, dynamic relationship between apostles and churches, with the authority of the apostles coming from their closeness to the revelation in Jesus Christ.

Eventually this apostolic role was refined into the offices of bishop, who was seen to have oversight and primacy, and presbyters or priests to whom the bishop delegated powers of presiding at the eucharist and administering baptism. A host of minor orders and functions were developed and formed into a hierarchy which serviced both the local and the wider church. Initially bishops were chosen by the laity and consecrated by bishops from other communities, so as to link the local and the catholic, but this involvement of the local church through the laity was to be reduced to the signifying of consent in the liturgy of consecration.

EXERCISE

What images of ministry do you form from your reading of the New Testament?

What gains and losses do you think were made in the increasingly hierarchical nature of ministry?

Development of clericalism

By medieval times the role of ordained ministers had shifted significantly. In his book *The Shape of the Ministry*, Hugh Melinsky (1992, p. 65) describes this shift:

> The twelfth and thirteenth centuries also saw a fundamental shift in the understanding of ministry not uninfluenced by feudal concepts. Originally the *titulus ecclesiae* was the local Christian community to which a man was appointed by his ordination. Canon 6 of the Council of Chalcedon made it quite clear that a man could not be ordained *in vacuo*: 'No man is to be ordained without a charge, neither presbyter, nor deacon, nor indeed anyone who is in the ecclesiastical order ... ' This ruling was valid down to the twelfth century. In 1179,

however, the Third Lateran Council radically reinterpreted the term *titulus* to mean the guarantee of a livelihood. No doubt some such financial provision was needed given the chaos of previous centuries, but this step served to sever the old link between call and community.

Furthermore, now that almost everyone was baptised, the boundary between 'church' and 'world' shifted from baptism to ordination. As a result, priesthood was seen more as a personal state of life or status than as service to and in a community. Ordination conveyed *potestas* (power), and this individualistic view opened the way to practices like private masses which would have been unthinkable to early Christians. This process was aided by a convenient semantic shift from *corpus verum Christi* to *corpus mysticum Christi* (from 'the true body of Christ' to 'the mystical body of Christ'). In the ancient church it was universally held that a man was ordained to preside over the former, meaning the church community; in the Middle Ages the terminology slipped into the latter, meaning his presiding over the eucharist. In brief, in the early church a minister was appointed to preside over a community, and so naturally he presided over its eucharist; then in the thirteenth century he was ordained to preside over the eucharist, and he might not even have a community over which to preside. The consequences of the change were drastic.

This change was reinforced in many ways. First, the insistence from the late eleventh century that priests should be celibate set the clergy apart to a very different lifestyle.

Second, ordination became a sacrament, giving a person an inalienable status which they did not possess before; this is the basis of an ontological understanding of priesthood. Ordination changes the person's being indelibly. 'Once a priest, always a priest.'

The practice of only the priest receiving the consecrated elements is a third reinforcement. The eucharist came to be seen as essentially the action of the priest, with echoes of Old Testament understandings of the distance between God and his people, which only the appointed priesthood could bridge.

Fourth, private masses, which would have been unthinkable in the early church, became a common practice.

Fifth, penitence and absolution became increasingly important in individual spirituality, with the bishop or priest being the person with the power to absolve. (Origen had held that laity could be endowed with the power to absolve.)

Sixth, legal and political developments reinforced the notion of the clergy as a separate caste with their own rights, privileges and responsibilities.

Nonetheless, in medieval times the laity retained considerable influence in the local church in England, through the power of patronage and through the guilds, chantries and fraternities which employed priests and were responsible for sophisticated systems of pastoral care, liturgical observance and private prayer.

EXERCISE

How do you react to these changes in the Middle Ages?

Can you see influences of these changes in ministry today?

Reformation

Luther is famous for proclaiming the doctrine of the priesthood of all believers. The Reformation made great strides in undermining some of the worst abuses of clericalism, stimulating a recognition of the value of all kinds of vocations, clerical and lay, among women as well as among men. Most Reformed churches still recognised the need for order and a special ministry for preaching, for the exercise of authority, and as a touchstone of the authenticity of the church's life and message.

They tended to retain the link between ordained ministry and eucharistic presidency, although as a functional and representative role, rather than any ontological notion of the minister embodying in himself special powers by virtue of the rite of ordination. The eucharist belonged more clearly to the whole community, with the minister being set apart to be a president rather than a priest in the cultic and medieval sense.

This development was accompanied in Reformed and Catholic churches by a renewed emphasis upon the importance of the minister being trained and educated so as to be effective not just through their office, but through the exercise of personal qualities too.

In England the Reformation settlement included the abolition of the monasteries and of the complex system of minor orders and associations which played such a key role in the medieval Catholic church. The result was that with the renewed emphasis upon the minister being a person of education, able to proclaim an intelligible faith in the vernacular, and the fact that within a few years the established church moved to a largely graduate ministry, the basic model for experiencing public ministry shifted from a collaborative effort involving a range of people and offices to a much narrower focus on *the* minister, with some assistance from churchwardens and others. Although clergy could be married, they tended to live apart in a 'clerical' household, separated from most of the laity by a university education.

The historian Patrick Collinson (1990, p. 254) writes as follows:

> In Protestant communities a new clericalism arose in the person of the godly preacher and pastor, an austere and remote figure living in the bosom of his family, and in his well-stocked study, emerging to denounce the sins of his congregation from the full height of the pulpit.

The status and education of the parish clergy made them natural magistrates, overseers and teachers.

The rise of the professions in the nineteenth century exacerbated this tendency for there to be one, trained, properly competent priest/preacher/pastor in each local community, and others involved in the life of the church tended increasingly to be seen as volunteers and assistants. This development was similarly reinforced by the establishment of theological colleges for the separate education and formation of clergy.

EXERCISE

What are the advantages and disadvantages of a professional public ministry?

Identify any signs that these developments have established a culture in which all those who seek to recognise any kind of ministry are led to feel that they too needed special training and authorisation?

How do these changes relate to the two images considered at the start of this chapter?

Contemporary debate

In recent times, the Roman Catholic theologian Edward Schillebeeckx (1980) has examined the evidence in the New Testament and early church and has argued that each Christian community has a right to a priest, and that public ministry is defined and validated not by the orders and status of the ordained, nor in the power to consecrate and absolve conferred by ordination, but by the quality of their 'priestly' *relationship* with the community they serve.

This makes ordained ministry dependent upon being rooted in the priesthood of the local Christian community and not something imposed on it from the outside. Such a style of thinking has enormous implications for the selection, training and sense of identity of a public minister. Schillebeeckx (1981) sees the medieval developments outlined above as something to be corrected, not least because the church in the modern world displays many of the features of the early Christian communities. It is small scale, more self-consciously local, pluralistic, and lives in a culture where absolutist ways of thinking are questioned and the relational is paramount.

EXERCISE

How do you evaluate the respective merits for public ministers of:
- quality of relationship with the community;
- authorisation from outside;
- an office which stands for being 'set apart'?

What would you like to reform in terms of our understandings of public ministry? Give your reasons.

Some images

Three images which highlight the developments outlined above are the maypole, the flagpole and the tentpole.

Maypole

In the medieval church there were a large number of offices and posts concerned with church and community life. Those in formal public ministry included not only the local priest but also monks and nuns, friars (travelling preachers) and a host of minor orders. Similarly the system of chantries and fraternities provided a framework for a great deal of what we would call lay ministry.

Thus many people had roles and functions in the life and witness of the church, all carefully organised in the hierarchies so beloved of medieval feudal society. The picture is that of a maypole, with people holding a range of different strands and operating in the dance of life in a carefully practised pattern, which allowed all to contribute appropriately while holding together an amazing variety of activities and concerns. Those in formal public ministry took their particular places in this complex arrangement.

The authority and identity of those in public ministry depended upon a system of orders, a role given by the church with clear functions and boundaries.

Flagpole

This is an image for the post-Reformation church. The Act for the Abolition of Chantries in 1538 destroyed the parish system as a collaborative and highly participative enterprise. With the abolition of monasteries and the minor orders, all major ministerial responsibility was focused on the mono-minister: the trained, educated, articulate agent of 'the word'. Laity increasingly became consumers of this professional ministry, which now stood like a flagpole in each community: bearer of the signs of the gospel and the authority of the word. Everyone else took their reference points from the flagpole.

The authority and identity of those in public ministry depended not so much on the system of orders (now much reduced) but upon the particular skills and abilities of each minister to preach God's word and to focus faith in parishioners' lives. The flagpole is the image of the one who oversees local life.

Tentpole

With the growth of other professions, those in public ministry became more narrowly clerical in their role and identity, a profession of their own. The industrial revolution produced a culture of voluntary consumers, and this became the mark of the church. Now the mono-minister became not so much the flagpole to whom the whole community looked up, for direction and focus, but rather the tentpole who bore the increasing weight of maintaining the church as an institution in a hostile and uncertain world. There are many offers of assistance, but in a professional culture all these lay contributions must be managed and controlled by the trained public minister. They become the tentpoles who are increasingly buckling under the weight of expectations which were associated with previous images but are unrealistic in the modern world. Although many laity have a significant stake in church life, for example through synodical systems, they remain volunteers who tend to look to the tentpole to give everything shape and strength.

EXERCISE
How do you evaluate each of these images?

Design an image which would be more suitable for the contemporary church as you know it.

Other professions increasingly operate through teams, mixing specialists, administrators and others as appropriate. Can the church learn anything from such models, or are they inappropriate?

EXERCISE
📖 **Read Paul's letter to Titus.**

Make notes about his main teaching in regard to the nature and purpose of public ministry.

Here are some features of the passage for consideration:
- Paul emphasises the importance of being chosen and commissioned as a leader.
- Titus is to put things in order by appointing (choosing) elders in every community; public ministry has a responsibility for order.
- An elder must have an exemplary public life, and this includes the family.
- An elder or overseer must be able to proclaim a message which agrees with 'sound doctrine'; the theological framework is not set locally but by the greater church.
- There are a great variety of ministries in the community, but all Christians need to grow in their vocations through continuing instruction.

- In such a culture those who learn from the sound doctrine which is taught will become teachers themselves at an appropriate level, but all depends upon a relationship to the authorised teaching of those in public representative office; thus the priesthood of all believers, the royal priesthood of Peter's epistles, flows from authorised instruction.
- In this way each Christian becomes an example and a teacher, through lifestyle and through the discipline of worship.
- The key is 'our great God and Saviour Jesus Christ, who gave himself for us to redeem us from all wickedness and to make us a pure people who belong to him alone and are eager to do good'.
- The world has its own systems and structures within which Christians should work creatively, making our own witness in relation to any shortcomings we perceive, and remembering that we are saved by grace, through the Holy Spirit, not through our own efforts; this is the mystery that the world needs to learn.
- The church must avoid disputes and arguments since we witness to a God of order and unity; public ministry is to focus unity as a manifestation of order.

EXERCISE
📖 **Re-read Paul's letter to Titus.**

How does this book influence your views on ministry?

What do you think?

Here are some further issues for consideration:

1. How does Paul's teaching about the role and responsibilities of those in public ministry relate to the historical developments outlined above?

2. Write a job description for a parish priest or local minister. Include how their tasks and responsibilities should best relate to others: church members and people in the community. If you are working in a group, compare your job descriptions. If you are working alone, it could be interesting to share your reflections with someone in public ministry. In either case, make a note of any further insights.

Further reading

Board For Mission and Unity (1986), *The Priesthood of the Ordained Ministry*, London, Church House Publishing.

Bradshaw, P (1983), *Liturgical Presidency in the Early Church*, Nottingham, Grove Books.

Carr, W (1985), *Brief Encounters*, London, SPCK.

Mason, K (1992), *Priesthood and Society*, Norwich, Canterbury Press.

Melinsky, H (1992), *The Shape of the Ministry*, Norwich, Canterbury Press.

Russell, A (1980), *The Clerical Profession*, London, SPCK.

5. MINISTRY TODAY

Introduction

We have traced some of the major developments in our understanding of personal and public ministry. In the present chapter we explore the relationship between these two aspects of ministry.

Reflecting on experience

Consider a game such as football, Scrabble or pass-the-parcel:
- What does the game require of its player if it is to be played properly?
- What factors or people other than the players are important, and why is this the case?
- What do these insights tell us about how creation works?

Personal and public

A key feature of current debates is the proper relationship between personal and public ministry. In 1987 the Church of England Advisory Council for the Church's Ministry (ACCM, 1987) produced a report now known as ACCM 22. It stated:

> The proper relationship between the ministry of the whole people of God and that of the ordained ministry joined in the service of God's activity in the world, has proved difficult for the church to maintain, not least at present. There have been constant tendencies for the tasks of one to subsume those of the other, so that in theory it is treated as 'the' ministry, whereas the two are actually *interdependent*, the health

of each depending on that of the other. Both together do what neither can do alone.

This notion of mutuality has been expressed in terms of 'collaborative ministry' and there has been a flowering of a considerable variety of other forms of authorised ministry alongside that of the parish priest. Since the 1970s there has been a development of non-stipendiary ministry (and more recently ordained local ministry or OLM). There has been a renewed debate in the Church of England about the role of readers, and the Roman Catholic Church has begun to train and deploy married men as deacons.

There have been considerable advances in forms of authorised lay ministry. Some, such as assisting with the chalice at Holy Communion, simply require the approval of the church authorities; others, such as lay pastoral assistants, bereavement and baptism visitors and youth club leaders, require training and some kind of local validation. These shifts have encouraged more team-working as a model of organisation and accountability.

EXERCISE
What kinds of authorised ministry, lay and ordained, can you identify in local churches?

What might such developments imply about the personal ministries of those who are not formally authorised?

Brief encounters

Some years ago I was waiting for the London train on the station at Bristol Temple Meads. I was wearing a 'dog collar'.

While I was waiting I walked along the platform and passed two schoolgirls who were sitting on a bench with files open on their laps. I went on and then wandered back towards the centre of the platform. As I stood waiting, one of the schoolgirls came up to me and said: 'Are you a vicar?'

'Yes', I replied. (In fact I was on the staff of a cathedral at the time, and not a parish priest, but the key thing is identification as 'a vicar'.) She went on, 'My friend and I have got two exams today at school and we wondered if you would come and bless us?'

I went back along the platform, talked to them about their exams, then I prayed with them and blessed them. The train arrived and I boarded. As we pulled out of the station, the schoolgirls were still sitting there revising. They looked up, grinned, and gave me the thumbs up sign.

EXERCISE

Write down your own reflections on this story, especially from the point of view of the church in the modern world.

How does this story relate to contemporary debates about, and strategies for, ministry?

Here are some features of the story for consideration. First, much pastoral ministry presupposes that we live in two worlds: an inner world of our hopes and fears and an outer world of the life in which we are set. Maturity and harmony come from trying to hold these two worlds together. Thus pastoral counselling or human friendship can be seen as important forms of Christian ministry.

However, my story challenges us to see that although the schoolgirls lived in two worlds, an outer world of exams and revision and an inner world of stress, desire to succeed, fear of failure, they did not come asking for help to hold these two things together. Rather they came and asked for a blessing. The search for wholeness is not about two things, it is about three things: the outer world in which we live; the inner world of our deepest feelings; and ultimately and mysteriously only something from totally outside of these two situations can give any real sense of wholeness and completion. This comes as sheer gift to those who desire it.

In one way, all Christians are ministers in these three ways, and the complementarity of collaborative styles of working and a greater variety of roles and skills being available means that we are well equipped to offer this range of care and counsel. Nonetheless it is clearly important in an increasingly secular world for those of God's children who stand outside of the churches to be able to recognise representative figures from within the Christian community who can be trusted to pray for God's blessing in times of need and in times of joy.

Thus the complementarity and mutuality which is so crucial to the design and delivery of ministry for those *within* the Christian church needs to be balanced by a clearly distinctive and distinguishable formal representative element who can be authorised to show and celebrate this public witness to the power and presence of God's grace in the ordinariness of everyday lives.

The second consideration is that such 'moments' of focus and connection for those who desire them need to be balanced by a much more widespread and comprehensive Christian witness in everyday environments, such as schools.

Thus for the schoolgirls, my particular and public ministry could be complemented by the witness of Christian teachers and pupils in their relationship with others, in their witness to the person of Jesus and the power of prayer, and in their example in attending public worship. Here we can see a myriad of more consistent and widespread ministerial activities being possible, each having the authority of its own freely chosen act of witness and concern.

This represents the possibility of collaborative working in the Christian community which is not simply locked into preserving the life of the church as an institution, but which is primarily concerned to be an agency for God's grace for the salvation of the world, the priesthood of all believers.

EXERCISE

How do you understand 'collaborative' ministry in the modern church? What are its strengths and weaknesses?

In your own experience, in what ways are people seeking 'moments' of blessing as they struggle to harmonise their inner and their outer worlds? Can you find examples of this search for wholeness in scripture? Choose two such stories and compare them.

Urbanisation

Recently I heard someone talking about the 'McDonaldisation' of the world, the development of a single capitalist culture. It is certainly true that despite the fact that millions live in rural areas, the predominant culture on our planet is one of urbanisation, of which 'McDonaldisation' is a part.

This shift poses enormous problems for an English religious culture which has been formed by the localness of the parochial system based on a resident priesthood. In Europe in the thirteenth century there was a similar challenge: contemporaries felt that they were facing the break-up of a stable parochial system focused on a settled priesthood (McGinn, 1998). There was a strong shift towards an urban culture at that time and the traditional parochial structures were found to be inadequate to deliver ministry and mission.

The response of the church focused on the foundation of the mendicant orders, the Dominicans and the Franciscans, and this provided a key to reconnecting with the growing urban culture.

Some of the key features of this new approach to ministry involved the following ten points:

1. Ministers became itinerant. The settled priesthood was complemented by a new order who concentrated on taking the word to the people (something Wesley was to do in eighteenth-century England).

2. This style allowed an openness to new ideas and forms of expression, particularly extempore preaching and the use of the vernacular.

3. The basic tool was ministration of the sacrament of penance. What those who experience the illusory freedoms of urban living, away from the settled constraints of small scale rural life, really need is *absolvere* – real freedom. Our urban world seems to have 'freed' itself from sin: there is little awareness of, or concern about, 'sin'. Yet guilt, brokenness and brutality abound. The friars preached a gospel of repentance and forgiveness, real freedom in a world of illusory freedoms, something objective and not simply relational. This is pure gift, nothing that human beings could construct.

4. The break-up of settled rural community led to enormous urban poverty, the downside of the attraction of materialism inherent in urban living. The friars chose to be poor, and thus to be counter-cultural, for the sake of those injured by and excluded from the excessive materialism of the times.

5. The friars modelled a new, flexible, but committed style of corporate living. They abandoned the traditional settled rhythm of corporate worship which had been the backbone of monastic

community and developed a more flexible pattern of common prayer. This proved to be an appropriate spirituality for urban dwellers too.

6. The spirituality of the friars emphasised the Passion of Christ and his real presence in the eucharist. As populations moved and institutions creaked, the emphasis was upon a person, not place and structures.

7. The development of third orders and confraternities enhanced the fostering of lay vocations while maintaining a proper loyalty to the Pope and the established church. This radicalism was controlled and clearly rooted in what the church had already developed.

8. There was a special emphasis upon education, and friars established influential centres in the major universities. One of the church's great resources in times of change and stress is education, leading people forward to new and greater perspectives. This required high-quality theological education for those becoming friars.

9. There was a strong alliance between the friars and the papacy, between new developments and established forms of authority and oversight.

10. The work of the parish clergy was complemented but not undermined.

EXERCISE
Make notes on your reactions to this thirteenth-century response to the forces of urbanisation.

Here are some issues for consideration:
- the need for new forms of ministry, rather than a gentle evolution of what already exists;
- the relationship between the settled pattern and the itinerant, flexible forms;
- the theological emphasis upon *absolvere* (objective freedom from sin and stress; freedom to receive new life) and the person and Passion of Jesus;
- the significance of some styles of ministry being clearly counter-cultural (for example, the dedication to poverty);
- a flexible approach to the disciplines of corporate life among Christians (for example, the possibility of services other than on Sundays);

- the need for education and new channels for lay vocations to be fostered.

Faith in the city

In recent years issues of urbanisation have been faced not simply with the traditional resources of Christian doctrine and established structures, but with sociological analysis and a concern for context. The emphasis is not so much upon 'teaching' as upon learning together, most especially from the needs and concerns of the poor.

The report *Faith in the City* (Archbishop of Canterbury's Commission on Urban Priority Areas, 1985, p. 106) states:

> An emphasis on the laity has been a strong theme to emerge in the written evidence submitted to us and in our discussions in the Urban Priority Areas (UPAs). There was a particular stress on the need for a laity in the UPAs committed to making Christianity take shape in the local culture. We strongly affirm that lay people have an important role in developing the mission of the local UPA church. They can present the gospel to others in a way that will make them feel 'this is for our sort of people'. Only those who are in, and of, a local area can say how God is speaking there. They can tell each other and the wider Church.
>
> Yet we have also had evidence that there are many obstacles in the way of developing an effective laity in the UPAs. They include the historical domination of leadership roles by those of other cultures, a concentration on words and books and equating intelligence and vocation with academic ability, a dependence on professionals and a degree of conservatism among the laity.
>
> To tackle such obstacles effectively, a 'bottom-up' rather than a 'top-down' approach is required. The structure of local churches should be more related to the tasks they have to undertake, which must be discerned and decided locally. The question is not so much 'How is the church to be run here?', but rather 'What are God's people called to be and to do here?' The answer to this question may we hope emerge from the undertaking of an audit for the local church, as we have suggested. Such a review may give rise to some disconcerting implications for aspects of church life. It may challenge existing views of the role of the clergy, the patterns and means of worship, the appropriateness of church buildings, and the allocation of resources.

Perhaps most of all it may lead to a serious consideration of how local lay leadership can be developed. There was a general recognition in the evidence submitted to us that 'the potential for local leadership is there and it needs to be sought, nurtured and encouraged'. A major emphasis in virtually all the submissions we have received is on the need for lay leadership to be developed systematically. Parishes repeatedly asked for training designed to reflect the experience, skills and cultures of local people.

A universal church crosses boundaries between ethnic groups, classes and cultures. At the same time, an authentic mark of the presence of the church in any particular place is that it should be rooted in the culture and character of that locality.

Here there are many resonances with the thrust of liberation theologies, rooted in the notion of 'base communities', which start not from traditional teaching from authorised personnel, but from personal experience and the daily concerns of people in the community. Scripture and tradition are interpreted through these lenses, and are a resource in so far as they nourish energy for and experience of 'liberation' in terms of human rights and opportunities. This is a more literal 'objective freeing' than the *absolvere* preached by the friars in the thirteenth century. The role of ordained ministry is supportive and enabling, rather than exhortatory and didactic.

EXERCISE
Compare this modern approach to that of the mendicant orders.

Here are some issues for consideration:
- the understanding of 'poverty';
- 'only those who are in, and of, a local area can say how God is speaking there';
- 'equating intelligence and vocation with academic ability';
- 'a "bottom-up" rather than a "top-down" approach is required';
- the strategy is an audit of the local church: freedom comes from within;
- 'an authentic mark of the presence of the church in any particular place is that it should be rooted in the culture and character of that locality'.

> **EXERCISE**
> 📖 **Read Exodus 32.**
>
> Make notes about the insights this story gives regarding ministry.

Some factors worth further consideration might include the following. First, Moses is formed as God's minister by his experience of the burning bush. God is present and yet absent, destructive yet not destroying. Moses learns to go up the mountain to a special set-apart place, to know God's presence and power more fully.

Second, Moses learns that he encounters the mystery of God not because of his own qualities or efforts but as the result of sheer gift.

Third, Moses' responsibility is to mediate something of this gift and this grace to God's people. He is called and commissioned to the priestly task of the believer: to help connect the people in their everyday lives to the purposes of God, to bring real freedom, *absolvere*.

Fourth, Moses was not good at ministerial skills. He needed Aaron to speak to the people. Aaron is called and commissioned to share in the public priestly ministry of Moses. This is an early example of collaborative ministry. Similarly Aaron is rooted more firmly in the 'context' of the people.

Fifth, all depended upon the discipline of going up the mountain to the special set-apart place. When Moses is delayed there, the people who simply receive the fruits of his ministry become impatient. They want a deeper connection with God there and then, to suit their own inclinations and needs. They will not wait.

Sixth, Aaron is lacking the wisdom and guidance of Moses, and thus he responds by using the material which is near at hand, and makes the golden calf. Ministry which uses human resources and human material becomes idolatry. The key ingredient is the gift of grace, which comes in the mystery of God's time and in God's way. For Aaron, ministry has become functional: to help the people worship and to allay their fears and celebrate their joys. What is lacking is the priestly component: mediating grace which is sheer gift.

Seventh, the people make great sacrifices of their precious possessions, but all was in vain. God fulfils his promises not at our beck and call but through the mystery of his chosen agents and his special places of encounter: outside the camp, not in its midst. Ordinary worship must be connected with these factors.

Eighth, whatever goes wrong in our religious life, *absolvere* is possible, through the one appointed by God to ask him for it, though there will be a cost. Passion is part of the process of absolution.

EXERCISE
📖 **Re-read Exodus 32.**

How does this chapter influence your views on ministry?

What do you think?

Here are some further issues for consideration:
1. What connections can you see between this passage and the development of the friars in the thirteenth century?
2. How can we best relate traditional forms and new ways, keeping our roots in what God has given?
3. What are the dangers we face today in personal and public ministry?
4. What is the place of particular people and special space within the ministry of the priesthood of all believers?
5. What can we learn from the passage about the place of local culture?
6. How do you connect incarnation ('bottom-up') with atonement ('top-down') in relating the responsibility of believers and the giftedness of grace?

Further reading

Archbishop of Canterbury's Commission on Urban Priority Areas (1985), *Faith in the City*, London, Church House Publishing.

Greenwood, R (1996), *Practising Community*, London, SPCK.

Messer, D (1992), *Contemporary Images of Christian Ministry*, Nashville, Tennessee, Abingdon Press.

Peterson, E (1995), T*he Gift: reflections on Christian ministry*, London, Marshall Pickering.

Zizioulas, J (1985), *Being as Communion*, New York, St Vladimir's Seminary Press.

6. WOMEN AND MINISTRY

Introduction

It is ironic that the word ministry basically means 'service': something historically associated with the role and function of women and yet, with a few exceptions, women have been excluded from public ministry until relatively recently.

Reflecting on experience

Compare a copy of a daily newspaper with a church newspaper. How are women portrayed in each? How are men portrayed in each?

Does your analysis provide an accurate snapshot in relation to the attitudes of modern society?

How does your analysis relate to the teaching of the Christian gospel?

Reflecting on women's experience

In the introduction to *Significant Sisters* Margaret Forster (1984, p. 2) writes:

> You cannot say you are a feminist in the same way you can say you are a Catholic or a Methodist. The only way to clear away the utter confusion surrounding the meaning of feminism is to start regarding it first of all as a kind of philosophy, as a way of looking at and thinking of life for all women.

It will immediately be obvious that this produces a problem: life for one woman is not the same as life for another. Even further, life in one place for one woman is not the same as that life in another place. An English feminist was never the same (and still is not) as a German feminist. All feminists think they want 'self-fulfilment' for women, but since that 'self' changes dramatically from country to country, from class to class, and from age to age, this ambition is almost meaningless. What *is* 'self-fulfilment'? Are there certain fundamental principles upon which all feminists can agree regardless of social, cultural and political differences? The history of feminism shows that there are but that it took a long time for them to be recognised. The trouble was that feminists did not know where to begin. They had the greatest difficulty in deciding *why* woman's lot was so much worse than man's even before they moved on to deciding how it could be improved. Long before active feminism arose, the theorists debated the situation and came to different conclusions. Some thought education was the key: women were not educated for anything but subordination. Change their education and their expectations in life would change. Others thought it was a matter of biology, that nature was the real enemy, and these were the most depressed theorists of all, for what could be done about nature? But while all this intellectual debate was going on, while the tracts and pamphlets on the condition of women were appearing throughout the eighteenth century, the first stirrings of *active* feminism were being felt.

EXERCISE

Margaret Forster writes that feminism 'is a way of looking at, and thinking of life for all women'. Should all women be feminists then?

Should the aim of feminism be 'self-fulfilment'?

Are there any fundamental principles upon which all feminists can agree?

Why was 'woman's lot ... so much worse than man's'?

The Christmas gospel: a mother and child reunion

On Christmas Eve in 1805, Frederick Schleiermacher, the famous German theologian, placed a special present on the family Christmas tree. It was a story to help those who heard it to think about the meaning of Christmas. In Germany at that time, presents were opened on Christmas Eve. They were labelled with the name of the recipient but not with the name of the giver. Part of the fun of Christmas was to guess who had given what! Schleiermacher's gift was to his family. They unwrapped the story and read it aloud.

Hark the herald angels sing: The story is of a family gathering round the tree on Christmas Eve. They discuss Christmas. One of the girls talks about the importance of music. Music is a more profound means of knowing God than mere words, so the angels sang in the heavens when Jesus was born. Similarly, many come to our churches to sing hymns at Christmas: bound in a deep communion, an atmosphere of worship and mystery. Words are inadequate to convey much about the Word. We need all our senses: thus the importance of music and worship, a word beyond words.

Unto us a child is born: Then the conversation moves to childhood. Unto us a child is born. The group discusses the differences between the sexes. For females (according to Schleiermacher), childhood is a time for games which prepare for adulthood: dolls, wendy-houses. As a result, women mature easily, almost naturally. Childhood flowers in homemaking, motherhood, womanhood. One of the party around the tree points out that it is different for men. Males rarely become the heroic figures of their playtime: thus maturity is a problem and in one sense men never grow up; they remain little boys at heart, finding fulfilment in games and hobbies around whatever adulthood brings. Unto us a child is born. What do we make of this child? How do we handle the child born in each of us? Is there a different agenda for male and female?

Gentle child of gentle mother: Finally the conversation moves to the nature of womanhood. Women are seen as more intuitive, able to handle things of the heart, the stuff of religion. Christianity is about the birth of the child: in us and for us, as the prologue to John's Gospel makes clear. How do we handle this life and all its potential? Is Mary a sign at Christmas that women have a special place in helping all of us accept something of the mystery of this gift of life: accepting, believing, trusting, focused in homemaking? After all, heaven is the home for which we live to prepare.

He who would valiant be: At this point the discussion is hijacked by two of the men, arguing about the historical truth of Christmas and the meaning of redemption. This conversation nearly wrecks the festive atmosphere. Men want to rationalise, control, put a handle on things: true religion and wonder are squashed by loud human voices. These children want to be heroes, not homemakers. The occasion is saved by a latecomer, Joseph, who refuses to join the theological argument and simply says that Christmas is 'one long, loving kiss that is given to the world'. The party ends around the piano, in music and song, and one of the girls sings. True religion is rescued from serious men: restored by women and children, the place it properly started.

EXERCISE
Reflect on the story presented by Schleiermacher.

Here are some issues for consideration:
- Is the Christmas gospel about the mystery of a mother and child reunion, for all of us?
- Consider the 'ministries' of women and men in the story. How do they compare with the analysis of Margaret Forster in her introduction to *Significant Sisters* and with your own experience of church life and church history?
- Some of the thinking was expressed in the nineteenth century in terms of 'the two spheres'. The sphere for women included sympathy, sweet ordering, the home, and influence. The woman was the moral and spiritual guardian of her family: the angel in the home. The sphere for men included creating, ruling, the world and power. Men were to confront the forces of the world and exercise power.
- These two spheres were seen to be complementary. Is this an accurate assessment? Has much changed in recent times? You may like to consider whether or not the Victorian fashion for wearing white wedding dresses continues to model this kind of relationship between men and women.

Maude Royden

An interesting and inspiring figure who can help us consider some of the key issues relating to women and ministry is Maude Royden (1876–1956). She was born in Liverpool and came from a shipping family. She went to study at Lady Margaret Hall in Oxford in 1896, a time when few women had opportunities for higher education.

Maude had a great gift for teaching and public speaking, but she found it very difficult to develop this vocation because of the constraints placed upon women being involved in such activities.

As a young woman she was invited by a friend, Hudson Shaw, to lecture on the University Extension Scheme. This was an attempt by the traditional universities to take further education opportunities to more people and yet, ironically, the authorities in Oxford were very reluctant to have a woman as a public lecturer. It was only when Hudson Shaw threatened to resign from his own pioneering work in the north of England that the authorities relented; they agreed that Maude could lecture in Oldham and Bury. We should note that this change was due to the insistence of a man already in the structures of power. Maude's vocation was totally dependent upon him.

At the beginning of the twentieth century she was involved with the Life and Liberty movement, part of a radical group of young Anglicans who wanted to change the established church to enable more participation in its life by ordinary members. The fruit of their work was the Enabling Act of 1919 which introduced a measure of self-government into the Church of England in the form of parochial church councils and synods.

During their campaign the group held a residential meeting at Cuddesdon Theological College, near Oxford. The Principal of the college, Jimmy Seaton, was a prominent member of the Life and Liberty movement, as were William Temple (at that time Rector of St James Piccadilly but later Archbishop of Canterbury) and Dick Shepherd (vicar of St Martin-in-the-Fields). This radical group, committed to greater participation in the church, met at Cuddesdon, only to be told by the Principal that Maude would not be able to sleep at the college since that was against the rules: she would have to sleep in Oxford. Despite vigorous debate, the Principal stood firm, the others reluctantly agreed and Maude left the meeting.

Here is another snapshot of the problems facing women in the area of vocation and ministry. Despite the radical views of these men in the

Life and Liberty movement about changing the church, closer to home they had a massive blindspot, conveniently covered by rules and rituals of long pedigree. Maude was powerless to change these 'institutional' factors that so easily blunted a radical vision.

Maude had a great gift for preaching, but because her own Anglican Church was reluctant to allow women into the pulpit, she developed her vocation at the City Temple in London (a Congregationalist church) and then at the Guildhouse, a project which she established with Percy Dearmer (a great liturgist) and Martin Shaw (a well-known musician). Maude became famous for her preaching, and introduced the opportunity for people to meet with her after the service to share their own views.

With regard to the process of change, Maude was clear that the official Church of England would not lead, but only follow, and thus she wrote in 1917 (Fletcher, 1989, p. 154):

> Someone must give a lead. My doing so will not prejudice but will help the cause of other women. The Church will regard me with horror and say what a lot of harm I am doing, but in the course of time it will begin to consider the possibilities of asking more religious and more modest women to speak in sacred spaces.

This provides another profound insight into the nature and process of change in relation to institutions: often it requires courageous and prophetic action by individuals to push back boundaries and to highlight new possibilities, which others can then see and follow.

EXERCISE
In the light of the story of Maude Royden, reflect on the following questions. To what extent do you agree and disagree with them?

Do good and radical men often have real blindspots about opportunities for women, conveniently clothed in established rules and rituals?

Do institutions tend to follow, rather than lead, in the area of women's vocations and ministries? ▶▶

> Is there a need for courageous and prophetic action by men from within the structures, and by women challenging the traditional boundaries?

The church and women

Maude Royden (1924) published a book called *The Church and Woman*. It presents a radical and challenging analysis of the issues facing the modern churches in the area of women in ministry. She begins by stating quite boldly that in human history the subordination of women to men is universal and constant. The whole of human history is a witness to this fact. Feminists who grasp at odd examples of women exercising leadership and breaking this mould are simply reinforcing the case, for such examples are only noteworthy because they are so rare. She writes:

> a candid study of the great civilisations produces the conviction that at no time and in no country have women been seriously regarded as the equals of men. (p. 12)

Maude Royden goes on to show that this is true of Israel in the Old Testament. There is a brief glimpse of the ideal in Genesis chapter 1:

> So God created man in his image, in the image of God he created them; male and female he created them. (p. 36)

But then from chapter 2 woman is clearly 'the helpmeet' of man, and this sets the tone for the rest of the Old Testament.

It is the same in the early church and the writings of St Paul. Despite the inspired insight in Galatians about 'neither male nor female', Paul does not really accept the spiritual equality of the sexes. For one great statement of principle, Paul gives us a dozen counter-claims in practical affairs. Thus, the head of the man is Christ, but the head of the woman is man. While man is the image and glory of God, woman is the glory of man. Paul, like all his contemporaries, accepted the spiritual inferiority of women. This was true of Jews and Gentiles, Greeks and Romans.

Maude Royden then takes the story to medieval times and argues that the emphasis upon celibacy and virginity led to an even deeper contempt for women, who are seen as unclean, temptresses, needing the spiritual models of Mary and monastic separation. Even motherhood is denigrated in medieval spirituality because Mary is honoured as virgin.

The Reformation could be seen as a glimmer of hope with the recognition of marriage as a vocation, but Maude comments wryly that the introduction of *obedience* into the marriage vows simply reinforces traditional views. Instead of being the 'helpmeet', woman becomes the 'holy helpmeet', the obedient helper in the home.

Thus she argues that the whole of church history, the whole of Christian theology, is at one with all known civilisations about the spiritual inferiority of women. She is blunt and realistic, with no special pleading and no manipulation of a few shreds of evidence to suggest alternative trends.

EXERCISE

What are the strengths and weaknesses of Maude Royden's analysis of history?

Can you outline an alternative reading of scripture from the one presented by Maude Royden?

Christ and women

Anyone concerned about seeing women positively in terms of the church would be dismayed by Maude Royden's arguments up to this point in the book. However she then turns to the subject of 'Christ and women'. She writes: 'Paul says that we must trust everything by this standard, by the standard of Christ, not human standards.' She shows that Jesus is unique among founders of the great religions in ignoring the 'absolutely universal assumption in his time about the inferiority of women to men'. Given his Jewish background and upbringing, this fact is truly amazing.

Jesus includes women in parables, in illustrations and in miracles, often when it seems unnecessary to do so, since an adequate example seems to have been given already. Maude develops an analysis of the Gospels which has only recently been taken up by the feminist theologians, to show that many parables and teaching illustrations are presented in pairs: a male example and a female example. This use of 'a double example' is especially prevalent in Luke, but evident elsewhere too. Maude argues that this method was unusual and in one sense unnecessary, but it provides an amazing contrast to the culture in which Jesus stood.

Similarly in the story of Martha and Mary we find for the first time in history a religious teacher rebuking a woman for being too much absorbed in her domestic duties (service). She sees Jesus' rebuke of Martha as the charter of women's freedom, since Mary is commended for choosing the better part. Maude notes the irony that ever since that moment the church has been trying to take this better part away from women.

Finally Mary Magdalene is given the good news of the resurrection, the foundation of the Christian gospel, and commissioned by Jesus to take this message to the apostles. They do not believe her. Jesus is dead, they revert to their cultural norms and see a woman as an untrustworthy witness. In Christ's lifetime there was a brief glimpse of light regarding the role and potential of women, treating the women the same as men and sending women out to proclaim the resurrection, but as soon as he is dead the denying culture takes over and the male disciples are back where they started, with the spiritual inferiority of women.

Maude goes on to ask if the church had been wrong about women. The answer is not a simple 'yes'. This would be too simplistic. Jesus promised that the Holy Spirit would lead us into all truth. She goes back to Paul's inspired vision in Galatians 3:

> there is neither Jew nor Greek,
> there is neither slave nor free,
> there is neither male nor female;
> for you are all one in Christ.

In his own time Paul only dealt with the first part of this agenda: the race issue. It has continued to challenge churches, but Paul put it firmly on the map of Christian theology. This left the class issue (slave and free) and the sex issue (male and female). Maude holds that the class issue in the West came to the fore in the eighteenth century with the witness of William Wilberforce, and has continued to be recognised as something of major concern with debates about socialism and the notion of a third way.

The one part of Paul's inspired vision which the churches had not yet tackled was the sex issue. For Maude this needed to be the primary agenda for the twentieth century. She made her own witness and was active in campaigns for women to have the vote and to gain other rights and opportunities.

EXERCISE

What are your reactions to Maude Royden's assessment of the New Testament?

Look at the Gospel of Luke and try to identify some of the double examples in Jesus' teaching.

Is the 'sex issue' the key one for the contemporary church? How would you weigh this concern against those of race and class?

Look at your answer to question 8 in the Ministry Questionnaire and make notes about how it relates to some of the ideas and issues raised in this chapter.

EXERCISE
📖 **Read Luke 1:1 to 2:7.**

Make notes of your reflection about women and ministry in this narrative.

Here are some points for consideration.

First, the question 'What will this child be?' is asked of the infant John. It is the question asked of every baby: will she be like her mother, her father, her grandparents? The New Testament is partly written to answer this question in relation to John and then to Jesus: 'What will this child be?' Will John be a great figure in Israel like his father Zechariah? Will Jesus be a great leader like his ancestor David?

Second, the New Testament was written by men whose concern in answering the question 'What will this child be?' focuses upon male roles of leadership, kingship, oversight, victory, power, success. These are the frameworks used to interpret Jesus and John: prophet, priest, king, lord, teacher. These are images about power, status and achievement.

Third, the two mothers disappear from the narrative very rapidly. Both are largely silent figures. They bring to birth the life given by God into the world, through the painful and bloody process of childbirth, from which comes new life. That is the secret of motherhood.

Fourth, we need to pay more attention to the mother. Elizabeth was blamed for her barrenness. In those days it was simply the woman's fault. So she had lived in a social wilderness, almost hidden. Then the miracle of pregnancy and birth. Immediately Elizabeth disappears: she is self-effacing. And who is John like? What will this child be? John lived in the wilderness; he is self-effacing: 'I am not worthy to undo his straps', 'I must decrease, he must increase'. He calls others to be the same: 'Have fewer shirts, be content with your pay, be self-effacing and give space for God.' John is not like his father, a great achiever in Israel, an important figure in Israel. He is like his mother, self-effacing and meeting God in the barren wilderness. John is wild and unconventional: just like an older woman having a baby unexpectedly.

Fifth, Mary was also a self-effacing mother: a poor peasant girl, empty (virgin) and unmarried but willing to give space for the gift of God's life through the unconventional and extraordinary. She remains a silent, largely background figure once the birth has taken place. Mary too is self-effacing; God's purposes come first. And who is Jesus like? What will this child be? He is not a successful leader in the house of David: Jesus refused to be made king. Jesus is self-effacing: 'not my will, but thy will be done', 'I cannot judge between you', 'one is coming who will do greater things than I'. Jesus lives in the wilderness, in the background, constantly moving on, going into hiding. Jesus is not like his father. Jesus is neither like God, the great ruler of the universe, nor David, the model king of Israel. Jesus is like his mother, self-effacing and meeting God in the bustle of everyday life or in the quiet wilderness.

Sixth, this narrative warns us of the danger of moving too quickly from the miracle of the birth of God's life into the masculine world of power and achievement: the story of a baby becoming a man. This sets up a pattern for vocation and ministry which can easily miss the point of God's new life being made manifest among us. The key to the question 'What will this child be?' lies in the mystery of motherhood and the self-effacing solitude which has been the lot of women throughout human history.

What do you think?

Here are some further issues for consideration:

1. What are the strengths and weaknesses of the interpretation of this narrative?
2. To what extent might such an analysis be unfair to women, and

likely to reinforce traditional stereotypes about a ministry of service and being on the margins?

3. How does the gospel challenge the cosy patriarchal culture of the New Testament and the tradition of the church?

4. 'What will this child be?' How should the Christian frame an answer to this question in the light of issues raised in this chapter? What does your answer say about 'women and ministry'? Could it be argued that women have a more naturally 'priestly' ministry if the latter is seen in terms of helping to give birth to the life of God in us and among us (see John 1)?

Further reading

Byrne, L (1995), *The Hidden Voices: Christian women and social change,* London SPCK.

Clark, E and Richardson, H (eds) (1996), *Women and Religion,* San Francisco, Harper.

Fletcher, S (1989), *Maude Royden: a life,* Oxford, Blackwell.

Forster, M (1984), *Significant Sisters,* Oxford, Oxford University Press.

Furlong, M (ed.) (1984) *Feminine in the Church,* London, SPCK.

Hebblethwaite, M and Storkey, E (1999), *Conversations on Christian Feminism,* London, Fount.

King, U (1989), *Women and Spirituality: voices of protest and promise,* London, Macmillan Education.

Loades, A (1987), *Searching for Lost Coins: explorations in Christian feminism,* London, SPCK.

Reuther, R (1983), *Sexism and God Talk,* London, SCM.

Storkey, E (1985), *What's Right with Feminism,* London, SPCK.

7. ORDER AND AUTHORITY

Introduction

In the nineteenth century the forces released by the French Revolution towards the freedom of the individual and the questioning of traditional social and political hierarchies began to crystallise around movements for democracy and the full participation of equal parts: equality, fraternity, liberty.

While recognising the richness of this movement, religious and political leaders were confronted by the problem of how to maintain systems of order and authority, so that some kind of structure and stability could be maintained alongside the increasing demand for individual freedom, whether in terms of political rights or of vocation and ministry. This issue still constitutes a major agenda for all societies and social institutions.

There have been a number of radical solutions proposed by Christian groups, solutions based upon charismatic experience and fluid forms, and making a direct appeal to the New Testament accounts, but these movements tend to flourish only in small groups and the principles are not easily applied to larger communities. St Paul can be seen as someone trying to address this same agenda of order and authority as the Christian church expanded so rapidly.

In this chapter we shall examine some of the ideas of Charles Gore (1853–1932), who explored ways of learning from St Paul, honouring the traditions developed by the church, recognising the importance of the individual, and valuing the 'oneness' of the church catholic.

Reflecting on experience

Identify an example of tension between individual aspirations and the claims of an institution for order and authority to take precedence.

• Describe the case from the point of view of the individual.
• Describe the case from the point of view of the institution seeking to give priority to order and authority.
• How do the vocations of individuals and of the church relate to each other in your own experience of church life?
• Who decides, and by what means, when there is a conflict?

Expectations

I was rushing to catch a train, having been held up by traffic on my way to the station. As I bought my ticket there were three minutes to go before the train was due to depart. As I hurried along the platform towards the subway I was stopped by a dishevelled man, who looked like some kind of homeless beggar. My heart sank. I had only two minutes to get across the station for my train. The thought maliciously crossed my mind, 'What great rigmarole would he try to tell me to show how deserving he was? Would it be the one about his elderly mother being seriously ill in Edinburgh and he just needed ...?'

I certainly did not have the time or the patience to endure it, yet I had to. I stopped, expecting the worst.

'Are you a vicar?' he asked.

'Yes', I said warily (I was wearing a dog collar).

Then, instead of launching into a great narrative about his bad luck and his need for the fare to Scotland, he simply said, 'I'm Bob. I've had a breakdown, been on the streets, but I'm getting better slowly. Here's a pound, please put it in the collection and pray for me.' Then he was gone. I was left clutching his £1 coin. I continued down the subway and boarded my train just before the doors were locked.

Bob was an extreme example of the confusion and stress which engulfs so many of us in the modern world. What he most wanted was reassurance:

• that there was a structure of order and authority;
• that he could reclaim his place of stability and security within it;
• that there was a church which stood for this saving reality;

• that there was a person who could represent this church and who could pray for him, joining him to the vehicles of salvation.

EXERCISE

If you could have a conversation with Bob, what would you want to ask him and what would you want to say to him?

Do individuals need structures of order and authority to avoid chaos, or is such a need a sign of weakness and immaturity?

Charles Gore

Charles Gore came from an aristocratic background: he was the grandson of an earl. Thus he appreciated the importance of order and authority, though not uncritically. Authority could only be exercised effectively when it was freely given approval and assent. He had a profound influence upon William Temple and Michael Ramsey, and thus is a key thinker for the contemporary Christian church. Gore advanced the following key ideas:

Idea 1: God's creation is teeming with variety. There will be an inevitable spectrum of experience and belief. This is evident in the New Testament and in the early church.

Idea 2: The mechanism to establish order is not by one voice claiming a special authority (which was the ground of his criticism of Roman Catholicism) but by what he called the 'comparing of independent testimonies'. This was the purpose of the great ecumenical councils in the first four centuries: to compare the different experiences of grace and to challenge local accretions to the gospel by a commitment to share a common doctrine about the person and work of Christ.

Idea 3: Within this process God calls out particular people to exercise particular functions. Of primary importance in testing the authoritativeness of the gospel and the development of Christian ministries are the apostles and their successors, who share in the task of maintaining the 'mould' in which all Christian experience is tested (Romans 6:17).

This 'mould' is the story of Jesus' life, death and resurrection, to which the apostles and their successors are called to be primary witnesses.

Idea 4: All Christians are endowed with 'reason'. This is not simply the human ability to think, but the light of Christ which flickers in each person and is the source of them discovering their own true vocation and ministry. 'Reason' is given in various ways and is part of the spiritual blessing on those called and commissioned to apostolic leadership in the church.

Idea 5: The use of 'reason', the development of the light and life of Christ in each person, is to be nourished and shaped by the four key resources ('the mould') provided by God for the making of his church: scripture, the creeds, the two sacraments of Holy Communion and baptism, and episcopacy.

Idea 6: Scripture is primary:

> The early church, believing the Bible to be the guide of individual Christians in faith and conduct, would have all her members well versed in its contents. They could safely read the scriptures for themselves and be earnestly exhorted to do so, if only the church's teaching had first given them the right point of view for their study. Thus guided by the mind of the church, they were bidden to see for themselves whether the whole teaching of the church was not to be found in scripture. Thus the familiarity of the whole body of the people with the original record would serve to maintain a scriptural tone and keep the church's current teaching and system from deterioration. (Gore, 1905, pp. 62–64)

In this way scripture was a resource for each individual and local church, but only as each is part of the corporation of the catholic church. Scripture is the resource of the whole Christian enterprise, as well as the resource of parts within it.

Idea 7: The apostles and their successors form a collegiality which gives real unity to all the diverse parts of the church. Similarly in any one area, the apostles' successors (bishops) or those appointed by them to positions of oversight (*episcope*) give focus for the unity of Christian experience: in testifying to the authentic and authoritative story of Jesus living, crucified and risen (the creeds); in standing guarantee to the authenticity of the order and form of sacramental worship; in upholding the primacy of scripture as resource for every part of the Christian enterprise.

Idea 8: Individual believers will explore their own vocation and ministry by: seeking God's will and guidance (each Christian remains a learner); testing their experience of God's grace against the 'mould' of sound doctrine entrusted to the apostles and their successors; trusting that the order and harmony of the church is an important witness to God's order and oneness; and hence desires for change and development will be contributed in a suggestive rather than in an imperialistic spirit.

Idea 9: Doctrine is a focus for the living experience of God. The indwelling Spirit ensures that the great Christian doctrines of Incarnation, Trinity and Atonement are not simply formulas to help us understand past events, but ordered and authoritative structures for interpreting human experiences of grace, forgiveness and new life. This is another reason for emphasising the importance of a dynamic relationship between each individual believer and the corporation of the church focused in its duly called and authorised leadership, whose primary responsibility is to help test and enrich all human experience in the context of the great doctrines developed by the church for this purpose.

Idea 10: There will always be room for new insights about Christian behaviour and belief, but these need to be explored, tested and negotiated in ways that maintain rather than destroy the order and authority of the wider church.

Idea 11: This notion of order and authority presupposes a hierarchical organisation giving priority to the catholic over the local, the apostolic faith over individual experience, the oneness of the church over desires for development, and the vocation and ministry of the church over that of individuals and smaller groups.

Idea 12: This was realistic according to Gore because most lay people need great latitude within which to explore vocation and ministry in terms of appropriate beliefs and behaviour. Each individual needs space within which there can be growth, change and development. This essential and God-given freedom, however, requires an overall framework which guarantees the centrality of the great Christian doctrines about the life, death and resurrection of Jesus: focused in creeds, sacraments, scripture, and entrusted to an apostolic ministry.

Idea 13: Such a notion of order and authority as the essential structures for salvation implied a particular discipline to which all Christians must be subject. For Gore these were: a distinctive creed, distinctive worship, distinctive moral law, and distinctive social life. These provided a practical framework within which vocation could be properly nourished and ministry exercised. The forms of each distinctiveness were to be established by the dynamic of appointed leadership, lay participation, doctrinal fundamentals and scripture described above.

Idea 14: Christian vocation and ministry would generally emerge from a long and serious period of training. Without such careful preparation the foundational order and authority of the church would not be properly appreciated or utilised. Gore worried about cheap and nominal grace.

EXERCISE

What are the constraints and freedoms provided by Gore's understanding of order and authority?

How do you observe variety and oneness being held together in your experience of church life?

Gore sees the four key resources of the church as scripture, the creeds, the two sacraments, and episcopacy. What would you add to, or subtract from, this list? Write down your reasons.

Gore advocates the importance of the apostolic ministry in guaranteeing, through this divine gift, the authenticity of the gospel as it is presented in various times and cultures. Are there other ways of safeguarding this authenticity?   ▶▶

> Democracy tends to start from the authority of each individual and builds order from the bottom-up (that is, by consensus). The Christian church has started with the authority of the gospel and the church, and built order within which individuals can find an appropriate freedom. Can you reconcile these different approaches, or advance a rationale for favouring one of them?

Distinctiveness of Christian ministry

Gore called Christians to the highest standards of moral and social life, as the primary context for ministry. In his book *The Reconstruction of Belief*, Gore (1926, p. 777) argues that Christianity is 'primarily a way of life to be lived by a community'.

> Thus when the Church of the New Covenant went out into the world, the first name of it was 'the way'. Its primary function was to exhibit among men a new way of life, a new kind of fellowship with God realised in a new kind of fellowship of men. People talk disparagingly of a 'merely ethical gospel', and contrast it with the Gospel of the New Testament. Quite rightly. The new law for the Church was warmed and inspired by a gospel about God and redemption, about Father and Son and Spirit, which made it something very different from a mere code of ethics. But nevertheless it was primarily as a way of life to be lived by a community, claiming to be both the true Israel and the New Humanity, that the religion of Christ went out into the world and converted men. The bulk of the New Testament is ethical teaching. It describes and enforces 'the way'. Even in the most doctrinal epistles this will be found to be surprisingly true.

> EXERCISE
> Christianity is 'primarily a way of life to be lived by a community'. What does this insight imply for your understanding of vocation and ministry?

In his 1891 Bampton Lectures, Gore (1891, p. 212) had argued even more passionately:

What I am complaining of, what I want you to complain of, with a persistence and a conviction which shall make our complaint fruitful of reform, is not that commercial and social selfishness exists in the world, or even that it appears to dominate in society, but that its profound antagonism to the spirit of Christ is not recognised, that there is not amongst us anything that can be called an adequate conception of what Christian morality means. The prophetic function of the church, as it seems to me at the present moment, is not so much, in the first instance, to expand Christian influence as to concentrate it: to see to it that all men, whatsoever be their own convictions and practices, shall at least acknowledge what it is that a Christian must believe, and how it is that a Christian must live and act at all points where he touches human life.

There must be produced a clear acknowledgement of what it is that a Christian must believe. We must strive to purge from all accretions the current presentation of the Christian creed, and to rid it of all that can bring it into conflict with the legitimate claims of reason, or seem to limit the freedom of enquiry or of criticism. We must so preach our creed as to 'commend ourselves to every man's conscience in the sight of God'. But when we have done our best to effect this, the Christian creed will stand out, as in past history and in scripture, so in the preaching of today, as a distinctive intellectual position, in regard to which a man may be in one of many different attitudes, but ·the general meaning of which he can hardly fail to apprehend. In the same way we must have all men acknowledge how it is that a Christian must live. We want the Christian moral law, the law of purity, of brotherhood, of sacrifice, to be as intelligibly presented and as clearly understood, as the dogmas of the Christian creed. We want it worked out with adequate knowledge in its bearing on the various departments of human life. In a word, we want a fresh and luminous presentation of the Christian moral code and some adequate guarantee that one who is deliberately, persistently, and in overt act, repudiating its plainest obligations shall cease to belong to the Christian body. 'Do not ye', writes St Paul to the Corinthian Church, 'judge them that are within, whereas them that are without God judgeth? Put away the wicked man from among yourselves.'

Gore believed that the church had suffered a major disaster by the mass conversions which followed the age of Constantine.

EXERCISE

'We want a fresh and luminous presentation of the Christian moral code and some adequate guarantee that one who is deliberately, persistently and in overt act, repudiating its plainest obligations, shall cease to belong to the Christian body.' How important are boundaries of behaviour and belief for Christian ministry? How might such boundaries be clarified and upheld?

Similarly the distinction between 'respectable and disreputable sinning' had become a matter of considerable scandal. In the book he wrote for the Home University Library in 1929 called *Jesus of Nazareth*, Gore (1929, p. 69) stated:

> In every settled society there tends to grow up a distinction between respectable and disreputable sinning. Certain kinds of sins are 'scandalous'. They tend to upset the decent order of society; they 'outrage morality', by which is meant the accepted standard of orderly and decent living. Such sins are murder and violence and theft, and blasphemous or atheistical language, and adultery or open sensuality which desecrate the home life. Other sins, though they may be formally regarded as sins, are tacitly condoned or taken for granted. Now, no one can read any one of the Gospels without perceiving that Jesus absolutely refused to recognise any such distinction between respectable and disreputable sins. Nothing is more evident than that in his eyes the love of money, selfishness, contempt of others, pride, uncharitableness, are at least as bad as violence or adultery or fornication. Nay, he regarded the sins which are scandalous in the eyes of society as in this sense less spiritually dangerous than the respectable sins, that the latter are harder to repent of and to forsake. 'The publicans and the harlots', he said to the highly respectable Pharisee, 'go into the Kingdom of God before you'. No doubt some writers, not only in our own age, have misused the fact that Jesus was specially alive to the danger of 'respectable' sins, as if it meant that he was lenient or comparatively indifferent to those which are commonly 'disreputable', in particular that he condoned or lightly regarded sexual sin. But this is not the case. But when he did talk about sensual sin, it was with a simple severity. One of the few occasions when he gave a plain answer to a plain question and spoke with dogmatic authority was in asserting the indissolubility of the marriage tie.

All Christian ministry should reflect this emphasis upon a distinctive practice.

EXERCISE

Jesus 'regarded the sins which are scandalous in the eyes of society as in this sense less spiritually dangerous than the respectable sins'. Do you agree? What might be the implications of this argument for discerning and deploying gifts in 'ministry'?

Thus for Gore, the Christian vocation was not simply about discerning the gifts and responsibilities of each individual: the call and commission of the community came first. There was a corporate order and authority that was prior to, and determinative of all Christian ministry.

These marks of Christian 'distinctiveness' were to inform and shape every individual ministry, and those in public office were required to emphasise this overall reality and its rootedness in the living, dying and rising of Jesus as focused in scripture, sacraments and creeds.

In *The Body of Christ* Gore (1901, p. 323) states:

> Baptism puts at our disposal new spiritual power for our personal life, but it does this because it incorporates us into society. And the new 'member', thus incorporated, proceeds either at once or, in the case of an infant, as his powers mature, to receive his full citizenship in the New Jerusalem by his 'sealing' in confirmation. This laying on of hands again conveys an individual endowment: it is the strengthening of the individual life by the gift of the Holy Ghost. But it is also a social ceremony with a social meaning. It is outwardly a benediction from the chief officer of the society, and it conveys to the confirmed his full right in the royal and priestly body. From very early days it was accompanied by anointing: it was at least called an 'unction' from St John's days. This meant what the early medieval ritualists expressly stated, that the member on whom hands were laid was being consecrated king and priest, consecrated, that is, to his full civic and religious rights. This primitive idea makes thoroughly reasonable the novel ceremony of our present Anglican rite, which associates with confirmation the formal acceptance by the now responsible individual of the moral duties of his Christian position. But we have lamentably let slip the accompanying idea of the lay priesthood and citizenship, an idea

so essential to that reform of the church on really representative lines which is so widely desired, and for which confirmation ought to afford so significant a basis.

He goes on to emphasise Augustine's teaching about the corporate aspect of Holy Communion which has flowered in the modern liturgical movement. Sacraments are corporate activities with social implications.

EXERCISE
'We have lamentably let slip the accompanying idea of the lay priesthood and citizenship.' If the sacraments embrace us in 'corporate activities with social implications' what might this mean for vocation and ministry, for the place of baptism, and for participation in Holy Communion?

EXERCISE
📖 **Read Romans 6:1-23.**

Make notes of your reflections about order and authority in relation to this passage.

What do you think?

Here are some points for consideration:
1. Christian vocation and ministry springs from 'being buried with Christ by baptism', an initial denial of our 'natural' human state since this is fallen and imperfect. Vocation is gift, not a simple development of apparently innate abilities.
2. To be baptised into Christ Jesus is to be made one in him.
3. There is a clear distinction between 'yielding yourselves to sin or to God'.
4. Vocation and ministry manifest Christ's new life: they are agents of resurrection, enemies of sin, harbingers of his life.
5. This presupposes a discipline of self-examination against the story of Jesus, focused in scripture, creeds, apostles and sacraments.

6. The method is to 'become obedient from the heart to the standard of teaching to which you were committed' (verse 17). The teaching of the church is primary, formative, determinative.
7. This discipline and obedience paradoxically 'sets us free' in the service of righteousness (verse 18), which is, of course, our earlier definition of ministry.
8. Such ministry comes not from our endeavour, but as 'the free gift of God' to those who submit to this discipline and obedience.

Further reading

Avis, P (1992), *Authority, Leadership and Conflict in the Church*, London, Mowbray.

Boff, L (1985), *Church, Charism and Power*, New York, Crossroad.

Council for Mission and Unity (1996), *Visible Unity and the Ministry of Oversight*, London, Church House Publishing.

Gill, R (1989), *Competing Convictions*, London, SCM.

Gore, C (1905), *Roman Catholic Claims*, London, Longmans Green and Co.

Platten, S (1997), *Augustine's Legacy*, London, Darton, Longman & Todd.

8. CATHOLIC AND LOCAL

Introduction

The church has always tried to give order and shape to the outworking of the vocations and ministries of the baptised, and to recognising God's presence and power in those who stand outside of the formal institution. Often this has been achieved by some kind of hierarchy, for instance the order of deacons, priests and bishops, which developed in the early church. Throughout church history there have been attempts to give more freedom for the forces of prophecy and charismatic leadership, generally in tension with established structures and systems.

Reflecting on experience
How long has it taken (or will it take) for you to feel a full member of the community in which you live or work? Why is this the case?

Think of an example where 'differences' between people cause conflict and problems.

Think of an example where 'differences' between people become the source of richness and strength.

How can 'differences' cause these contrasting outcomes?

Tension

This tension is almost inevitable. The church was launched with Jesus' words at the end of Matthew's Gospel (28:19):

> Go therefore and make disciples of all nations, baptising them in the
> name of the Father and of the Son and of the Holy Spirit.

Hence there is a single gospel for all people. And yet, on the day of Pentecost, each person heard 'them telling in our own tongues the mighty works of God' (Acts 2:11). The gospel is both universal and particular, catholic and local. Hence it requires both an institutional framework and a sensitivity to the uniqueness of each individual.

The first preaching of the gospel produced a number of separate churches, in contact with the message of the apostles as delivered by Paul, and recognising his authority because of that apostolic call and commission. Nonetheless each Christian community developed according to local gifts, conditions and opportunities.

Only as the church increased in size and scale did it become necessary to take steps to ensure an essential uniformity in the key doctrines of the faith, and a basic compatibility of practice. This 'institutionalisation' of the gospel inevitably took the form of the culture in which it was set, the Roman imperial model. Thus order was based upon a hierarchy of offices, and a clearly defined system within which each vocation found its proper fulfilment. The result of this development was that the 'local' became firmly subservient to the catholic. This was soon reinforced by a common Latin liturgy and text of scripture.

The Reformation marked the beginning of an attempt to reclaim a place for local uniqueness and variation, both for places and for people. In many ways we live with the tensions between local and catholic identified so clearly in the sixteenth century. Political developments towards democracy, and in some cases socialism, have created a strong impetus for egalitarianism within church life, in terms of equality of opportu-nity and a fully participative system. This impetus lies behind some of the documents quoted in chapter 1 seeking to explore the full significance of the priesthood of all believers and the ministerial responsibilities of each baptised person. It was in response to such developments that Gore advanced his case for order and authority.

In a culture which is suspicious of institutions and almost uncritically affirmative of the individual, the traditional church emphasis upon catholicity is under siege, though there is limited resource in our traditions to provide an alternative that does not lean largely towards a strong central identity at the cost of the local.

EXERCISE

Look at your answer to question 4 of the Ministry Questionnaire. What does this variety of ministries say about the issue of 'catholic' and 'local'?

What is the balance between 'catholic' and 'local' in your own experience of church life?

How can personal vocation and ministry best be reconciled with the notion of 'one Lord, one faith, one baptism, one God and Father of us all' (Ephesians 4:5)?

What are the advantages and disadvantages of democracy for Christianity?

Should the institution or the individual take priority in the discernment and development of vocation and ministry? Give reasons for your answer.

Roland Allen

Roland Allen (1868–1947) was a missionary in China as a young man, and then a vicar in the Diocese of Oxford. He resigned over the issue of baptism, feeling that it should only be administered to those who showed evidence of faith. He enjoyed a long and fruitful retirement, spending his later years in Kenya with his son. His view was from outside of the establishment, rooted in the realities of the missionary situation where Christianity had to establish itself in a hostile environment. This perspective, which links him to the experience of much of the Anglican Communion, has proved to be prophetic of the situation that has developed in England since the Second World War, and crystallised clearly in the 1960s. It is interesting that Allen predicted that his ideas would not be taken seriously until the 1960s, and with the initiative to explore non-stipendiary ministry at the end of that decade he was proved right.

The movement of his thought can be traced through the titles of his three most significant publications: *Missionary Methods: St Paul's or Ours?* (1912), *The Spontaneous Expansion of the Church* (1927), and *The*

Case for the Voluntary Clergy (1930). Like Gore, his work was rooted in the New Testament, but in contrast to the amazing breadth of the former's interests, Allen concentrated upon a minute analysis of the Acts of the Apostles and the Epistles, to produce very creative, but somewhat detailed and occasionally repetitive works outlining his vision of 'making church' from a missionary perspective, and predicting that this approach was going to become increasingly relevant in England.

Roland Allen makes five main points relevant to our theme of catholic and local. First, a key text for Allen was John 7:38–39. Jesus said on the last day of the feast, 'If anyone thirst, let him come to me and drink. He who believes in me, as the scripture has said, "Out of his heart shall flow rivers of living water." ' Now this he said about the Spirit, which those who believed in him were to receive: for as yet the Spirit had not been given, because Jesus was not yet glorified.

Pentecost marked the gift of a new Spirit, the Spirit of Jesus. This Holy Spirit is distinctive in the way that Jesus was distinctive, and it filled the apostles with a consciousness of power, a recognition of the needs of others for this power, and an impelling desire to connect these two things by proclaiming the gospel of Jesus. Each individual is blessed with this Spirit in responding to the message in Acts 2:38, 'Repent and be baptised in the name of Jesus for the forgiveness of sins, and you will receive the gift of the Holy Spirit.'

Those who received this Spirit were impelled to preach this gospel to others, to convince them of a need for repentance, forgiveness and a new spirit, this Spirit of Christ. Hence baptism was no longer a symbolic washing away of sins as that practised by John the Baptist: it was baptism into Jesus Christ, and it brought new life and new power for the individual who received it.

This was not to deride the significance of those who expressed God's love by offering a cup of water to the thirsty, but it was emphasising that besides such charitable expression there was a new Spirit that could be received through this process of repentance, forgiveness and new life.

Second, Allen takes the 'newness' of the Holy Spirit with radical seriousness. This Spirit impels mission and cannot be contained by structures of church or of theology, for the latter always come second to the missionary impulse of the Spirit. Hence those who receive this Spirit are driven by a creative dynamic into a continual process of making church.

The apostles in Acts 'administer the Holy Spirit' to others. They do not invite people to join a group or conform to a theological scheme:

they administer the Holy Spirit to individuals who are moved to receive it. And, unlike the Old Testament where individuals are given a special spirit for particular work, in the New Testament the Spirit is in the whole body of Christians, uniting and impelling everyone in a common enterprise. Thus the common life is exalted to heights previously reserved for those who did some special work for God. Ordinary people are filled with the Holy Spirit for their common daily life as Christians, and this provides a revolutionary exaltation of every individual and a revolutionary significance to the common life. Christians are not a chosen people but a royal priesthood: all Christians are kings, priests and prophets, and from this reality stems the radical possibilities for making church which Allen comes to propound.

Third, Allen studies Acts to show that doctrine and structure always followed the essentially missionary impulse of the Spirit. Peter is impelled to go to Cornelius, and this unprecedented encounter with Gentiles is blessed by an outpouring of the Spirit upon them all. Jew and Gentile learn new things together about the power and purposes of God, and from this impulsion of the Spirit the Council of Jerusalem recognises the consequent changes to doctrine and practice for the church. Such is the power of the Spirit to lead into new things, that the scriptural command for circumcision to be the mark of the Covenant can be changed. The Spirit led the apostles to sense power within themselves, to recognise the need of others for this power, and to connect these things by proclaiming the gospel of Jesus. The result is a new outpouring of the Spirit for themselves and for others, and a remaking of 'church'.

Mission comes first as the primary force of the Holy Spirit; ministry and order come second and subsequent. This is a process Allen had experienced in the mission field, while recognising that the 'established' understanding of Christianity with which he and others were involved inclined them to put ministry and order first, so that mission became conformity to these established ways of making church, and not a radical openness to the new things of the Holy Spirit.

A fourth point is that in the making of church, the source was the key (that is, the moving of the Spirit), not the consequences. Thus when Peter and Paul are challenged about their work with Gentiles, their defence is the impulse of the Holy Spirit, and 'church' is remade around a reality which they and all Christians were able to taste. Hence Christian action is not limited to the probable consequences which worldly wisdom might foresee: it is to be rooted in the impulsion of the Spirit to know power in oneself, the need of others for that power, and the gospel of Jesus being proclaimed to connect these two things.

Allen felt that the contemporary church was too concerned with possible consequences, and thus trapped in conservative management of what seemed to have been achieved. He did not claim that looking to the Spirit made discerning the truth easier, but it led to different priorities: worship not synods, prayer not discussion.

Thus, fifth, mission will not produce conformity to what the church thinks she knows, it will always produce new styles, new revelations, distinctive insights into the gospel. The problems of harmony and understanding are the signs of a healthy church. Moreover the fact that the Spirit impels a common life and evokes radical newness means that the primary focus for this to be manifest is not in individuals, nor in a large universal or national church, but in a local Christian community.

The Holy Spirit, as Acts illustrates, is a mould-breaker, not a mould-maker (just as Jesus himself was a disturber of established religion). This moves beyond the dynamism of Gore's 'moulding' process in its openness to new things, in positing a much more radical understanding of the making of church, in relation to the role of the individual's vocation and ministry, in recognising the limitations of the institutional, and in advocating the key mediating role of the local.

However, Allen insists that it is the Spirit who takes risks, not individuals or groups, and this is the guarantee of proceeding in such a manner. The Spirit of Jesus is not limited by his earthly revelations.

Allen developed the following dictum:
- The Holy Spirit of Jesus constitutes us in the church.
- The Holy Spirit of Jesus will equip us to be the church.
- We are to trust the Holy Spirit of Jesus.

Christians are good at giving the Holy Spirit credit after an event: they need to trust this Spirit beforehand too.

EXERCISE

How do you evaluate Allen's notion that the impulse of the Spirit is primary, then church order and theology follow?

What might be the dangers of Allen's challenge that the church becomes too concerned with possible consequences?

The making of church

We continue with Roland Allen's case for the importance of the local by examining seven additional points. First, mission works on the principle of the difficulty of keeping a secret. Mission is spontaneous, unorganised and impulsive in human beings who cannot refrain from sharing what is the source of their values and beliefs and behaviour. Spontaneous expansion begins in normal human interactions, and in sharing the source of this new life, it is intensified in debate and exploration. Just as love grows through sharing and being focused in signs and sacraments, so in the Spirit sharing renews both the sharer and the person shared with. This impulse is the work of amateurs; those who are paid to say things lack this credibility. Hence the importance of laity and voluntary clergy, though Allen retains a role for stipendiary ministers too.

Sharing the life of the Spirit renews the past, exposes ignorance and one's own need to know and reflect more, and is thus the key to continuing nourishment. Being a missionary is a necessary way of life for each Christian.

A second point is that this spontaneous expansion and outreach will cause problems. Allen says that you cannot trust people, but you have to! Christian life is about teaching and learning, not controlling and knowing. This explains why Paul could establish so many churches in such a short space of time.

> We are in greater danger of serious disorder when, in fear of freedom we restrain a God-given instinct, than when we accept the risks of giving it free play. (Allen, 1927, p. 16)

Because of this essential element of spontaneity the local church must be self-supporting, self-extending and self-governing. The national church is not to determine the local church: rather the mould-breaking nature of the making of church will give space for the local church to be genuinely local. This is not congregationalism because there is an equally essential dynamic between the local and the greater church.

However, to give space for the Spirit, Christians must not be bred into a culture of dependence, unconfidence and inarticulateness, such as Allen saw happening in the mission field through undue emphasis upon what the home church thought it knew.

Third, when people became Christians in an area, and received the

Holy Spirit in baptism, then those who had administered this Spirit to them should give them the key elements by which this new life is nourished and focused. These elements are the creed, the scriptures, the sacraments and the ministry.

The creed is the tradition by which all exploration is to be measured. Each member must be able to say 'I believe' (not 'I understand').

All must revere and wrestle with scripture. The uneducated will be given as much insight as the educated. The Bible is for the whole church and belongs to all Christians.

The church must be taught to administer and receive the sacraments. Allen (1926, p. 149) wrote, 'I have a profound belief in the power of sacraments' to teach and nourish at many levels. We must not try to teach all we know about them, we must give them, offer some insights and guidelines for their practical use and leave others to be taught through them. (The source, not the consequence, is the key.)

Ministers must be ordained if the church is to have proper order and government. Paul's pastoral epistles show that he chose people of good moral character and standing in the community, natural leaders who were ready to confess doctrine as it was given. The necessary qualities are those of 'life and speech', which are the only measure of an inward call. It is the church as a whole who receives officers, not officers who receive a church. The church as a whole is responsible for the good conduct of her officers and for order and government. Nonetheless leadership is important. Allen used to say that where there are three people there is a leader, and this reality needs to be recognised. Hence all will have vocations and ministries but there is a key role for leadership, accountable to the whole church, local and catholic.

Having given these gifts, the bishop and the missionary should leave the new church to use them as a means of learning to be the church in that place.

Allen's fourth point is that the bishop and the missionary (or stipendiary minister) do not abandon the local church to congregationalism. Paul's letters show him equipping local churches with these four essentials, leaving them to learn to be the church in that place, but engaging in continual dialogue with them about all kinds of matters. The Spirit of Jesus in apostles is given to oversee and authenticate the making of church, as it is in those trying to be the church in a particular place: and the Spirit of Jesus calls for co-operation, exploration and interchange. Church is made by a dynamic between the centre and the local, although the latter has more freedom and more overall responsibility than that allowed by Gore. The dynamic between the local and the greater church is important for both. Within it individuals have different roles, but always within a corporate endeavour.

Fifth, the local church is the primary organisation by which ordinary people experience God's grace, and thus must not be unduly or inappropriately overshadowed by a more 'universal' agenda. If the local church has the creed, the Bible, the sacraments and the ministry, it is equipped to be the place for nourishing and administering the Holy Spirit. Moreover it will use these gifts for the edification and expansion of the church along natural human lines of communication, local interacting in human living. This natural localisation will allow the gifts and energy of the Spirit to meet genuine local agendas through the vocations and ministries of Christian people in their everyday lives, whereas a more centralised system tends to give the local church an agenda unrelated to local particularities and to local gifts.

Through these suggestions Allen was advocating that God is not to be known simply in the personal and the universal (which only the institution can connect), but also in the local: a model akin to the early church where small-scale corporations were signs of the universal, a focus for the personal, but primary in themselves.

Doctrine will be the expression of faith that can continue to shape and feed lives, and offer connections with those outside. If doctrine becomes an oppressive agenda imposed from outside, Christians will become paralysed, confused, unconfident about sharing the faith, and eager to escape into the security of pastoral care which is not explicitly connected to the secret of the gospel. There will be a constant danger of heresy, but the Spirit of light lives in the darkness and we must trust that the darkness will not overcome it. Life comes from struggle.

Sixth, for these reasons Allen came to advocate a role for voluntary clergy, initially to provide an appropriate ministry for each local church, rather than leaving groups of Christians bereft of regular contact with the sacraments, the ministry and exploration of creeds and scripture. He appealed to the practice of Paul and retained his high church faith in a stipendiary priesthood by emphasising the need for dialogue between the local and the greater church so as to ensure that catholicity which is an expression of the Spirit of Jesus: joining all kinds of people in common enterprise. In this sense he valued the traditional Anglican structure of parish, diocese, national church, international communion. Paul maintained a dynamic interaction with local churches through 'the young men' (Timothy, Titus), through letters, and through personal contacts. This allowed theology as well as church order to be subject to this on-going dialogue, and provided a dynamic context within which the vocations of individuals could be developed, servicing local needs but accountable to the wider church too.

Further, following Paul's collegial working with what Allen calls 'the young men' and with local church leaders, he advocates the style of 'a college of priests who between them are responsible for the due conduct of services and the running of the parish'. Priesthood must be a model of the fundamental collegiality of the Christian enterprise. Paul seems to have appointed groups of local leaders, not just one person. Similarly, 'voluntary' priesthood was not part-time, such thinking makes a false distinction between spiritual and secular lives. For Allen it was rather a different way of enacting priesthood.

In the 1960s the shortage of stipendiary clergy in England began to provide a fertile ground for accepting some of Allen's insights about 'voluntary', essentially local clergy, though his willingness to risk abandoning strict standards of centralised training in favour of criteria for suitability being in terms of local recognition of gifts and leadership potential, has never been fully accepted by the established churches.

Seventh, and finally, in this way Allen advances a radical case for individual engagement and responsibility being taken seriously, since this is the material through which the Spirit works. Like Gore he balances this appeal to individual experience of the Spirit of Jesus with a high doctrine of the essential place of the corporation of believers as context and control. He agrees with Gore about the distinctiveness of the Christian life. However, he goes far beyond Gore. He charges each individual with the responsibility not just of contributing to the life of the church, but of being an active agent of mission, sharing the secret of the gospel. In addition he shifts the making of church from a dialogue between the individual and the resources of the institution (Gore's modified 'establishment model') to a dynamic between the individual, the *local* and the institutional.

Some steps in this direction were taken with the introduction of elected church councils but the significance of this use of the local as the *key* mediator between individual and institutional experience of grace was barely recognised by the 1960s. There has been a minor adjustment in some circles since then, though the radical (and biblical) resonances that might be possible have scarcely been explored: the desire for control and the safety of limiting authority to those in the hierarchy are too deeply entrenched. This is not surprising given the fact that since

Augustine's mission to England in 597 Christianity has been consistently imposed from above, established and centrally controlled.

However, the Spirit of Jesus may yet have surprises for us.

EXERCISE

How do you see personal ministry being embraced by the model of church advocated by Allen?

In what sense can 'each individual be an active agent of mission'?

What is the significance of non-stipendiary ministry?

Can you think of anything a local church needs at its heart besides the creed, the scriptures, the sacraments, and the ministry?

Allen claims that all churches should be self-supporting, self-extending, and self-governing. What are the advantages and disadvantages of such a proposal?

How does Allen's description of the church's life and task relate to your understanding of the modern term 'collaborative ministry'?

EXERCISE
📖 **Read John 7:37–39 and Acts 2:1–47.**

Make notes about what might be learned in relation to the relationship between the catholic and the local as contexts for vocation and ministry.

If we look at these texts in terms of Roland Allen's thinking we might note:
- the gospel of Jesus launches an enterprise to be continued and developed by his Holy Spirit;
- this universal gospel connects with people in their localness (their own language and culture) as much as in their individuality;

- scripture provides a common and connecting framework for interpreting the work of the Spirit;
- the story of Jesus living, dying and rising is the key to understanding both scripture and the Spirit;
- the impetus and call is to resurrection, though humanity in its sinfulness tends to crucify the life of God that is born in us and among us;
- the good news is that human repentance can open us to forgiveness and the fuller infusion of this new life; the key is baptism;
- the baptised will live out this 'risen' life in their own particular communities (localities), making it manifest by their fellowship and their charity;
- the focus is worship and table fellowship, the teaching of the apostles, the message of scripture, and the ministry of the apostles (compare Allen's list of the resources needed by the local church);
- there is a clear dynamic between local fellowship and witness, and catholic teaching and leadership;
- subsequently in the Acts of the Apostles there will be examples of individual vocations and ministries, but always pursued *within* this prior context.

EXERCISE
📖 **Re-read John 7:37–39 and Acts 2:1–47.**

How do these passages shape your views of ministry?

What do you think?

Here are some further issues for consideration:

1. How does the notion of the 'local' fit into the proper development of vocation and ministry for individuals and for the church as an institution?
2. What is the proper role of leadership, first in the local church and then in the catholic church?
3. How can we ensure that the story of Jesus living, crucified and raised up can be the basic factor for interpreting scripture and our own experiences in human life?

Further reading

Allen, R. (1962), *Missionary Methods: St Paul's or Ours?*, London, World Dominion Press.

Allen, R (1962), *The Spontaneous Expansion of the Church*, London, World Dominion Press.

Donovan, V (1978), *Christianity Rediscovered*, London, SCM.

Francis, J M M and Francis, L J (eds) (1998), *Tentmaking: perspectives on self-supporting ministry*, Leominster, Gracewing.

Green, M (1990), *Evangelism and the Local Church*, London, Hodder and Stoughton.

Long, C and Paton, D (eds) (1962), *The Compulsion of the Spirit*, London, World Dominion Press.

Warren, R (1995), *Being Human, Being Church*, London, Marshall Pickering.

9. SPIRITUALITY OF MINISTRY

Introduction

In this chapter we are going to look at the life and teaching of Evelyn Underhill (1875–1941). She became well known as a retreat conductor, spiritual director, theological lecturer, and writer on the spiritual life. She had a particular role in making the classics of Christian spirituality known to a wider audience by her work of translation and commentary.

Reflecting on experience
Many conversations are punctuated with phrases such as 'God', 'Oh my God', 'Jesus', 'Christ'.

They indicate surprise, wonder, fear: unconsciously people use this language when they stand on the border of prayer, of wondering, wanting and worrying.

Recall occasions when you have heard this kind of language, in conversations, novels or films, and consider what its use might tell us about God and about his children.

A praying presence

Maggie Vigor, who is involved in the ministry of prayer, offers the following reflection, drawing on Graham Greene's novel, *The Power and the Glory* (1971):

The wonderful paradox of it all lies in the way in which God uses the most ordinary for God's own special purposes. Just as we are fed in the mystery of the sacrament of God's precious body and blood through the ordinary stuff of bread and wine, so God uses the clay pots of ordinary people of no particular virtue save that they are called, to carry God's treasure and feed God's flock. As in *The Power and the Glory* (Greene, 1971), God uses the drunken priest 'to pass life on'.

> We are a pilgrim people, made of clay,
> Captives of our own greed and frailty
> And yet, we are the work of Your hands.
> You have made us in Your own image,
> And we bear within us Your Spirit of life,
> The seeds of immortality.

This paradoxical picture of the journey towards wholeness through brokenness, and mystery through ordinariness, is the more complete for us now that women as well as men are ordained priest. For women now, too, the priesthood is both at one with our whole humanity, and other, set apart through God's call and the sacrament of ordination. We too can become Christ-bearers, icons of Christ and channels of his grace in a new way and in our very being.

Priests are called, above all, to be present (for God, for people, for people before God) and to be witnesses of God's presence in and among us, ministering through God and for God as channels of love, grace and communication, through the sacraments, preaching and prayer, binding up the broken-hearted and bringing good news to the poor.

Each of us is caught up in the 'groanings and travails of creation' and has a particular part to play in building the Kingdom of God here on earth. Each of us will be caught up in suffering and joy of the 'divine consolation' in a different way, but we are all called to watch and pray, and we need consciously, constantly, to tune in our senses to attentive listening and watchfulness and waiting on God, for without God we are nothing, but with God all things are possible. God is faithful and will do it, not in spite of us but because of us.

> Give us, we pray, a stronger faith
> So that we may walk joyously into the unknown,
> An unshakeable hope
> So that we may comfort the despairing;
> And a love as vast as all the oceans
> So that we may hold all humanity in our hearts
> We ask this for the sake of Your love. Amen.

EXERCISE

What do you think Maggie Vigor has to say about priesthood as public ministry, about the priesthood of all believers, about women and ministry, and about the practice of prayer?

How do you understand the relationship between prayer, vocation and ministry?

Evelyn Underhill

In her book *Concerning the Inner Life*, Evelyn Underhill (1947, p. 4) wrote:

> We are drifting towards a religion which consciously or unconsciously keeps its eye on humanity rather than on Deity, which lays all the stress on service, and hardly any of the stress on awe: and that is a type of religion which in practice does not wear well. It does little for the soul in those awful moments when the pain and mystery of life are most deeply felt. It does not provide a place for that profound experience which Tauler called 'suffering in God'. It does not lead to sanctity: and sanctity after all is the religious goal.

This is a profound warning and challenge to an age which defines ministry as service but so often neglects the vital fact that the grace of salvation is sheer gift to those who are ready to receive it, attentive to their deepest vocation which is a calling from God. Thus all Christian ministry which is 'of salvation' (see the definition in chapter 2) will issue from the attentiveness we call prayer: the 'being present' referred to by Maggie Vigor in our first quotation.

Thus Evelyn Underhill (1937, p. 80) underlines this point in her book *The Spiritual Life*. She states that:

> the spiritual life will be decisive for the way we behave as to our personal, social and national obligation. It will decide the papers we read, the movements we support, the kinds of administrators we vote for, our attitude to social and international justice. For though we may renounce the world for ourselves, refuse the attempts to get anything out of it, we have to accept it as the sphere in which we are to cooperate with the spirit, and try to do the Will. Therefore the prevalent notion that spirituality and politics have nothing to do with one

another is the exact opposite of the truth. Once it is accepted in a realistic sense, the spiritual life has everything to do with politics. It means that certain convictions about God and the world become the moral and spiritual imperatives of our life; and this must be decisive for the way we choose to behave about that bit of the world over which we have been given a limited control ... Our favourite distinction between the spiritual life and the practical life is false. We cannot divide them. One affects the other all the time: for we are creatures of sense and of spirit, and must live an amphibious life ... Most of our conflicts and difficulties come from trying to deal with the spiritual and practical aspects of our life separately instead of realising them as parts of a whole.

The spiritual life embraces the personal and public ministry of every kind. However, this essential activity of prayer reflects some of the factors we have already noted regarding space, a variety of dimensions, the value of distance and the importance of roles.

In another work entitled *The House of the Soul*, Evelyn Underhill (1947, p. 47) uses the following picture:

We come back to examine more closely our domestic responsibilities: the two floors of the soul's house. We begin on the ground floor for until that is in decent order, it is useless to go upstairs. A well-ordered natural life is the only safe basis of our supernatural life: Christianity, which brought the ground floor, with its powerful but unruly impulses, within the area of God's grace, demands its sublimation and dedication to his purposes. We are required to live in the whole of the house, learning to go freely and constantly up and down the stairs, backwards and forwards, easily and willingly, from one kind of life to the other; weaving together the higher and lower powers of the soul, and using both for the glory of God. No exclusive spirituality will serve the purposes of man, called to be a link between two worlds.

Thus, to the eye of faith the common life of humanity, not any abnormal or unusual experience, is material of God's redeeming action. As ordinary food and water are the stuff of the Christian sacraments, so it is in the ordinary pain and joy, tension and self-oblivion, sin and heroism of normal experience that his moulding and transfiguring work is known. The Palestinian glow which irradiates the homely mysteries of the gospel, and gives to them the quality of eternal life, lights up for faith the slums and suburbs, the bustle, games and industries, of the modern world. Then the joys, sorrows, choices and renunciations, the poor little efforts and tragedies of the ground-floor life, are seen to be shot through, dignified and transfigured by the heavenly radiance, the self-oblivious heroism, of the upstairs life.

She warns of the danger of living in a spiritual bungalow, entirely bound up with the things of this world, and failing to appreciate that larger and more mysterious dimension which gives sense and direction to this human life. The bungalow mentality can easily become a ministerial spirituality which seems to be appropriate in the modern world.

Yet she also warns of the danger of trying to live in the devotional suntrap of the upper rooms, in a rarefied atmosphere so full of the things of God that there is no attempt to descend to the depths and engage with the practical tasks of the Kingdom coming amongst struggling humanity.

Underhill (1937, p. 88) wrote:

> The church is in the world to save the world. It is a tool of God for that purpose; not a comfortable religious club established in fine historical premises. Every one of its members is required, in one way or another, to co-operate with the Spirit in working for that great end: and much of this work will be done in secret and invisible ways. We are transmitters as well as receivers. Our contemplation and our action, our humble self-opening to God, keeping ourselves sensitive to his music and light, and our generous self-opening to our fellow creatures, keeping ourselves sensitive to their needs, ought to form one life; mediating between God and his world, and bringing the saving power of the Eternal into time.

Nonetheless, within this essential dynamic between divinity and humanity from which springs salvation, there will be different roles and responsibilities, which we will explore in the next section.

EXERCISE

Can the pursuit of 'ministry' become a focus which deflects us from attentiveness to its true author and sustainer?

What are the implications of living on 'two storeys' for our understanding of ministry? ▶▶

> Give examples from your own experience where 'The Palestinian
> glow which irradiates the homely mysteries of the gospel, and gives
> to them the quality of eternal life, lights up for faith the slums and
> suburbs, the bustle, games and industries, of the modern world.'

The Lost World

On the eve of her seventeenth birthday Evelyn Underhill wrote (see
Cropper, 1958, p. 4):

> I am going to write down this short account of my own feelings and
> opinions because I think that tomorrow will close a period of my life,
> and I want to preserve some memory of it before it quite goes away.
>
> As to religion, I don't quite know, except that I believe in a God, and
> think it is better to love and help the poor people round me than to go
> on saying that I love an abstract Spirit whom I have never seen. If I can
> do both, all the better, but it is best to begin with the nearest.
>
> If we are to see God at all it must be through nature and our fellow
> men.
>
> Goodbye sixteen years old. I hope my mind will not grow tall to
> look down on things, but wide to embrace all sorts of things in the
> coming year.

For the practice of ministry it became important for her to look
'wide' so as to 'embrace all sorts of things', rather than to 'grow tall to
look down on things'. This is an important element of the prayer
needed to enable vocation and ministry for salvation.

Evelyn Underhill was the daughter of a lawyer and married a
barrister. Evelyn, woman of the spirit, lived with men of the law. Con-
sequently she learned wisdom about the important dynamic between
freedom and restraint, between exploration and structures, between
mysticism and earthiness, and between individuals and institutions.

As a young woman she wrote a series of novels. Each has a similar
theme. In one of them, called *The Lost World* (1907), the hero Paul is a
young man who feels a deep call to be with God, to live as a mystic, to
pursue a deeply individual spiritual journey. However, at this same time
he feels a passionate, sensual love for a woman called Catherine. The
novel is about the struggle between these two forces: the higher path of
spiritual fulfilment and the lower path of human instinct.

In the end Paul renounces the call to the high road of mysticism for the lower road of marriage. On one level the story explores the fact that he seems like a Christ who fails to be crucified: he failed to give up everything for the glory of God. But the twist in the tale is that his call does not end with marriage, rather his call is simply worked out in a different and more earthly way. The novel shows that it is only by abandoning this lonely, heroic, higher spiritual path, that he can find a deeper spiritual maturity which he would never have achieved otherwise. The key is to pursue his love for Catherine and in a sense he is saved by the earthly love of a woman. He has learned to love the flesh, and not to despise it. True vocation and ministry involves the word being made flesh.

EXERCISE

How appropriate is the illustration of needing to live in a house, that is, on two levels, and maintain a proper intercourse between them?

How do you respond to the idea that God's call may often come in a lower key than we expect? Does God stoop much lower than we imagine, and desire us to engage similarly with the struggles and imperfections of humanness?

Is there a similarity between Catherine and the person of Elizabeth Bennett in *Pride and Prejudice*? Does Catherine perform a priestly ministry, albeit informally and unconsciously?

How might the practice of prayer enable us to better follow the Christ who himself took the road which went lower than the angels in order to offer salvation?

From mysticism to worship

Evelyn Underhill became a great spiritual teacher. Her first major book was called *Mysticism* (1911), her last major work was entitled *Worship* (1936). These titles chart her own spiritual journey from a very personal, individual quest to a positive engagement with the life and teaching of the institutional church.

She recognised the centrality of the personal experience of grace and the attendant spiritual disciplines, but she came to value the importance of history, tradition, public liturgy, doctrine and apostolic oversight as the key context within which an individual vocation was nurtured and ministry exercised.

She used a number of images to explore this understanding of the spiritual life. In one set of retreat addresses Evelyn used the picture of a great cathedral church with magnificent stained glass windows. She explained that if you simply look from the outside, the building may seem quite impressive but the windows will look dull and uninteresting. It is only if you go inside that you can appreciate the breathtaking beauty and realise that each window, in all its marvellous colour and construction, tells part of the story of Christ's living and dying and rising. You can see this wonderful and awesome story not just because of your own eyes, but chiefly because of the light which God pours through these structures and these stories.

The human task is to learn to go in and out of the cathedral. You cannot stay in the church because much else needs attention: the growing of crops, marrying, meeting, the earthly endeavours of humanity in all its complexities. But if you stay outside, you will fail to glimpse the glory which beckons, the story which speaks of salvation and the mystery of the light from beyond which gives life to the world: and without these insights human life will be dull, impoverished and ultimately meaningless.

She stresses that God is absolute light, too powerful to meet us directly, and thus it is through Jesus and his story that the light is mediated and made accessible. Thus prayer is not simply meditation on the issues of human living, nor simply contemplation of God: it comes from the mix and interaction of these things in the story of Jesus.

In terms of previous chapters we can note the following six points. First, there is a need for order and authority (Charles Gore). The cathedral provides a structure which can 'hold' the doctrines of the church so that people can come and be shaped by them. There is enormous freedom for those who come to be inspired to all kinds of beliefs and behaviour between their visits, but they remain focused on a common and catholic heritage.

Second, no doubt the cathedral needs its officers to maintain the structure and to help people interpret the stories they set forth. This might connect with our notion of an apostolic commission and the more formal, public exercise of priestly ministry.

Third, the cathedral is a special, set-apart place. People have to move from their own cosy worlds and travel some distance, both to reach it and to explore its resources. The notion of distance is important to the spiritual life, as is the resource of special 'set-apart' people, scriptures, creeds and places.

Fourth, the cathedral provides a place for catholic and local to be in dialogue. The impetus of the Spirit is rooted in the story of Jesus but takes people beyond this in ways most appropriate for their situation and their gifts.

Fifth, the cathedral is a witness to the unity which we have in God: a common creation, a common call, a common commission. However, its doors take us out into a myriad of cultures and challenges, each requiring its own particular ministries.

Sixth, the cathedral is a place of prayer where we learn something about presence, about the extraordinariness inherent in ordinary materials such as wood, glass and stone, about the dynamic between two levels of living, and about the challenge to be agents of that miraculous light in the dark places beyond.

EXERCISE

Evelyn Underhill warns us against laying 'all the stress on service and hardly any of the stress on awe'. How does the image of the cathedral help us to address this issue?

Structures can obscure light as well as protect and enhance it. What are the drawbacks of the cathedral image?

What might be the place of liturgy within this cathedral structure?

How can the necessary variety and flexibility of ministries be honoured and encouraged, since the 'cathedral' will inevitably encourage those who come regularly to place most value upon its own forms and practices? (This is the syndrome that many people who feel a call to 'ministry' feel the need to be ordained.)

EXERCISE
📖 **Read Luke 11:1–13.**

Make notes of your reflections about this passage in the light of some of the teaching of Evelyn Underhill.

Here are some points for consideration:

1. Jesus was praying 'in a certain place'. This is the spirituality of the set-apartness of space.

2. He was asked 'Lord, teach us to pray.' Prayer is a gift of Jesus, the life of the Spirit in us, not a human technique or discipline. It is something that occurs when we go to the Lord to learn.

3. Prayer begins when we acknowledge our dependence on God. All of us share this dependence for creation, sustenance, forgiveness and guidance amongst the perils and dangers of this world. There is always a greater dimension to acknowledge with thanksgiving. Human life needs to come out of itself into this marvellous light.

4. Forgiveness is central, both in our relationship with God and with each other. This is the truth proclaimed by the friars in the thirteenth century. Absolution is the miracle on which salvation depends. Ministry will always be a mediation of this miracle.

5. Real human need is the place where we meet Jesus in his needs. 'Because of his importunity he will rise and give him whatever he needs.'

6. We must learn to give because of need, not simply because of friendship. This is an essential element of ministry, in danger of being obscured in churches which are so centred on fellowship that all 'outreach' is to those within the Christian community. As Underhill made clear, 'The church is in the world to save the world: it is the tool of God for that purpose.'

7. Much of this work 'will be done in secret and invisible ways'. There is a danger in our present culture of professionalism and training that the only 'ministry' that we recognise is the formal and the official. The culture of the cathedral dominates and the mysterious working of grace in everyday encounters becomes obscured.

8. Yet we must learn to seek, to ask, to knock and to enter. This is the proper purpose of that cathedral structure: the place and the resources where we can seek, ask, knock and enter into more fully.

9. Each of us has an instinct to do good and not to give our children scorpions. Here is the basis and the bedrock for Christian ministry. Here is an innate goodness, a light that flickers in each human creature. Ministry as the 'ministry of salvation in the service of the world' happens inevitably and instinctively in all kinds of transactions.

10. Our instinct for goodness can be blessed by the Holy Spirit, so that we learn better to fight against evil and to follow Christ: the promise and commission of baptism.

EXERCISE
📖 **Re-read Luke 11:1–13.**

How does this passage influence your ideas of ministry?

What do you think?

Here are some further issues for consideration:
1. To what extent does 'dependence on God' form the basis of your understanding of ministry?
2. How can absolution be integral to ministry?
3. Where in your community is Jesus to be met in his need?
4. How can we learn to value and encourage ministry that is done 'in a secret and invisible way'?

Further reading

Greene, G (1971), *The Power and the Glory*, London, Heinemann and Bodley Head.

Nouwen, H J M (1996), *Can you Drink the Cup?*, Notre Dame, Ave Maria Press.

Underhill, E (1937), *The Spiritual Life*, London, Hodder and Stoughton.

Underhill, E (1946), *Collected Papers*, London, Longmans, Green and Co.

Underhill, E (1947), *Concerning the Inner Life with The House of the Soul*, London, Methuen.

10. MINISTRY TOMORROW

Introduction

We will examine two approaches to suggesting appropriate patterns for the future of Christian ministry in our culture. Both are directed towards the Church of England, but in fact deal with issues that are common to all the denominations in what is sometimes termed a 'post-modern' society.

Reflecting on experience
What have you noticed about local churches that seems to make them more or less likely to fulfil their aims in the next decade?

Collaborative enterprises

In an age which values individual liberty and its consequent pluralism, the future for Christian ministry seems to be in the direction of collaborative enterprises which recognise the importance of 'every member ministry'. This can be seen as one of the major thrusts in recent ecumenical dialogue, with an increasingly common commitment to 'the corporate priesthood of the whole people of God' (Council for Christian Unity, 1993).

Because the historical shape of church order and authority in the past has tended to be hierarchical, with the catholic taking precedence over the local and the individual, this movement has raised serious issues about these norms hitherto accepted as the proper interpretation of scripture and tradition.

The result can be a tendency to concentrate upon the ministerial tasks of the present, in terms of servicing the salvation needs of the world, and of those called to formal faith commitment, and giving particular attention to the effective management of these endeavours, with a consequent lack of real engagement with scripture or the traditional wisdom of the church.

Ministry becomes the charter and legitimate expression of a present-tense faith, and resources from the past, doctrinal, scriptural or structural, are drawn upon in an ad hoc manner, to bolster the current Christian enterprise as seems to be appropriate. Such resources are increasingly not seen as non-negotiable foundational elements for prayer and practice. This trend is exacerbated by the current emphasis upon local liturgical freedom which allows each worshipping community, and within it each worshipper, to make choices about their own particular spiritual diet. There is less public emphasis upon common prayer (except in terms of basic framework), upon set offices and a single lectionary.

A pic 'n' mix supermarket society (sometimes called 'post-modern') seeks a pic 'n' mix spirituality and the chief agenda is around the ever-increasing range of resources for this core Christian activity: ministry becomes a reflection of this culture – ad hoc, personal in focus rather than political, and rooted in the gifts and perceptions of the baptised as much as in the needs of the world in which we stand. This development has been encouraged by the phenomenon of 'compassion fatigue' in western societies, where media coverage can overwhelm us into a state of charitable inertia, able only to respond in small-scale, personal ways. It has also been encouraged by the increasing emphasis upon 'professional' standards in a wide range of ministerial practices, which disables all but those properly trained and accredited from much serious engagement beyond that of the ad hoc, personal response.

EXERCISE

Must Christian ministry always be a 'present-tense' activity, or can it be enriched and informed from the past?

Is it fair to caricature much contemporary spirituality as pic 'n' mix? Can you identify and expound any other types of analysis?

Should Christian ministry be 'political' as well as 'personal'? How do you understand these distinctions? ▶▶

> What are the advantages and disadvantages of 'professionalism' in the practice of ministry?

Robin Greenwood

The first approach to suggesting an appropriate pattern for the future of Christian ministry in our culture is illustrated in the work of Robin Greenwood, who was involved in the establishment of a Local Ministry Scheme in the Diocese of Gloucester, and then moved to be Ministry Development Officer in the Diocese of Chelmsford.

His two major books on this subject are *Transforming Priesthood* (1994), which explores a model of 'presidency' for ordained ministry, and *Practising Community: the tasks of the local church* (1996). We shall use material from this latter work to outline some of the key features in his thinking with regard to ministry.

Greenwood (1996, pp. 1–2) begins:

> This is a book about creative futures for the mission and ministry of the local church. My own experience and reflection is chiefly of the Church of England, but the issues raised here are generic to most churches today. The contemporary urgency to sustain and extend the mission of the church in each locality, together with a widening disregard for and cynicism regarding institutions, is leading to new insights about God's hopes for the church. The sharp context of present ecumenical debate and experiment on the identity and task of the Christian community includes a clear movement towards a theology of *communion*. In the search for a more adequate understanding of church the notion of *communion* speaks of a community of those who in unique and complementary ways are drawn into sharing in the mystery of God's gift to the world of Christ. The title *Practising Community* points to a threefold understanding of the task of the local church. First, as a doctor practises medicine, the church practises community, following the example of Jesus. Second, the sinful and divided Church has only the capacity for practice: it is far from achieving perfection. Third, this practice is not to create an insular community but rather to demonstrate and evoke, however partially, the practice of community in all the networks of society.

> This vision for the task of the church confronts a church culture currently in danger of being dominated by anxieties about finance and

steadily diminishing numbers of stipendiary clergy. The inescapable facts of the present day church are well known. In Church of England parishes and diocesan offices shortfalls in giving are bringing about situations for which there are no instant remedies. Those with a deep concern for mission often accuse senior church leaders of planning for decline. A more mature position is to recognise that calculating how to run a diocese with fewer clergy is partly an exercise of person management and financial adeptness, but also recognise that this is not the whole story. This book is written in the conviction that it is not sufficient to shore up the existing structures nor to maintain the inherited model of church. Rather, I share the belief that God is summoning the church to reframe itself by listening acutely to the new demands of mission and ministry at the opening of a new era. In a period of transition the hope that comes of commitment to prayer will be required while we live through the chaos associated with transformations of identity.

Greenwood (1996, pp. 5–6) sees the way forward for ministry in terms identified at an Edward King Institute Consultation in 1994:

- there is a biblical and theological imperative for collaborative ministry; it is not just fashion or a response to crisis;
- ministry belongs to the whole people of God by virtue of their baptism into Christ;
- there is a common calling to all God's people to share in the service (ministry) of their local church;
- the local church is the universal church present in each locality;
- the trinitarian understanding of God and the theology of the body of Christ point to a community of diversity in which all are entrusted with a ministry of costly reconciliation;
- the role of the ordained ministry is to serve and service the whole ministry of the people of God.

He advocates making the traditional parish system (sense of place) secondary to the 'redevelopment of the *idea* of the local church as a locally negotiated area of collaborative ministry' (p. 26).

EXERCISE
What is your own experience of 'collaborative ministry' in the local church? How do you evaluate it?   ▶▶

> To what extent can the 'idea of the local church as a locally negoti-
> ated area of collaborative ministry' take precedence over the
> importance of place and 'special space' which church buildings
> give focus to (as in Evelyn Underhill's image of the cathedral)?

Greenwood (1996) goes on to argue that the vocations and ministries of
each believer need to be brought together to most effectively serve the
needs of salvation in the community. The key is 'the community of
Christians ... rooted not only in the sacraments, word, and local fellowship, but in the ministry of the episcopate'. He goes on to recognise the
limitations of the traditional notion of set-apart overseers in particular
centres, and stresses that 'there is a sense in which all Christians are
bishops: all share in the episcopal office which for practical reasons is
focused in certain individuals. All are called. No one is redundant'
(p. 27). Here we see a radical desire to include and value every contribution for every function of the church's life and witness.

He points to recent ecumenical dialogue which has based this inclu-
sive understanding of the church upon the New Testament notion of
koinonia (communion) which:

> draws together a cluster of primary ideas: unity, life together, sharing
> at deep levels. Essentially to describe church as 'communion' is to
> speak of a network of relationships rooted in sharing a single reality.
> (p. 30)

The Trinity is the supreme sign of community.

> The church is called in Christ and through the Spirit, to model or be
> a sign of that communion which is the very being of God and the
> shape of his desire for the perfection of the cosmos. (p. 48)

Within this communion or *koinonia* Greenwood holds that:

> the most fruitful theology recognises that it is the local church as a
> body that comes before consideration of particular ministries.
>   Certainly local churches need the wisdom of itinerant apostolic
> clergy who bring new breadth to the local scene; but once resident in
> the local church those clergy should see themselves, as far as possible,
> as one with the local community, rather than semi-detached, even
> though, as we shall see later, that is not the whole story. (p. 53)

Here we should note the emphasis upon the local church as being the primary focus of catholicity, and the call for clergy to identify fully with it.

EXERCISE

'All Christians are bishops': the priest as representative of the formal *episcope* is to be servant and president among the people. How do you evaluate this vision with the arguments of Charles Gore for order, authority and hierarchy?

The local church has a primacy in relation to catholicity and apostolicity. How does this idea compare with the ideas of Roland Allen about an essentially dynamic relationship between local and catholic?

Thus, with regard to the central notion of catholicity and apostolicity, Greenwood (1996, p. 54) argues that:

> To be apostolic used to be a test of whether an unbroken mechanical link could be proved down the centuries between ordained clergy and the twelve apostles. A more accurate understanding in the light of present theological discourse is that, as catholicity is the whole local church community in relation to geographical world terms, apostolicity is to be in relation *through time*. The local church will be relating with the churches down the centuries that have witnessed to the life, death and resurrection of Jesus and also will be making connections *now* with the eschatological desire of God: 'The church manifests (apostolic) order and succession when its behaviour imitates the Lord's, when its teaching is faithful to the apostles' message and when its leaders are trusted exemplars worthy of imitation by all' (Mitchell, 1982).
>
> The sharing of the many to become one people of God who share in trinitarian communion in the eucharist and offer to the world a diagram of the Kingdom is a clear sign of the apostolic church. As such it needs no protection, dogmatism or strategies of domination. In vulnerability learned from Christ it is known for its ability and willingness to be companions with the weak and marginalised in society.
>
> In summary, apostolicity refers to the church's intimate connected-

ness with its past and its future. As the sign and foretaste of God's peace it is constituted both by its roots in the events of Jesus' ministry and the rise of the witnessing community and also in the eschatological wholeness of the Christ in whose hands the Father has placed the world's final destiny.

Here catholicity and apostolicity are rooted in the whole church, through the networking of local churches in communion. There is no notion of these factors being particularly focused in certain ministries for the sake of the whole, as we saw in Gore and Allen.

The local church holds these things together through the practice of 'collaborative ministry'. This is not some laity assisting the priest, but something best expressed in what has come to be known as 'local ministry'. According to Greenwood, the theology of mission and ministry that undergirds the development of local ministry is rooted in three principles which move beyond adversarial and dualistic relatedness towards deep mutual respect.

> The first step is a renewed understanding of baptism, supported by respected scholars of all major denominations, and experienced as authentic in the lives of many Christians. This emphasises that every committed member has a rightful share in the mission and ministry of the body of Christ.
>
> The second principle arises from a vision of collaborative ministry in which local churches regard themselves as corporate agents of mission, increasingly deploying local people in positions of leadership, and some would add, including where appropriate, ordination.
>
> The third principle is a view of the clergy, in both urban and rural areas, no longer as isolated and omnicompetent ministers, but as those who evoke and support collaborative Local Ministry Teams of many kinds. These principles lead to a radical revision of the shape of the ministry offered in, and by, the local church. (1996, p. 63)

Next Greenwood identifies five specific developments in the local church as a consequence of the radical revision of the shape of its ministry. These developments are as follows:

> Laity who are aware of themselves as the *subject*, rather than simply the *object*, of ministry. That is, to an acceptance of the responsibility of the whole people of God as the primary agents of Christian ministry, rather than being a group of people who are merely the recipients of ministry.

A body of clergy who act collegially rather than in isolation from the gifts of the laity and of other clergy.

Opportunities being developed for laity together with readers and clergy to engage in the whole spectrum of the church's mission. This would include church-focused ministries, but for the vast majority of laity it would be a recognition that the main focus of their ministry lies in the opportunities presented by their everyday responsibilities and challenges amongst the people and in the communities with whom they are engaged.

The realisation that groupings wider than a single parish, such as increasingly large benefices, deaneries, local ecumenical projects or locally negotiated groupings, are likely to be the operative agents of the local church of the future.

The recognition of the implications for training and educating clergy and laity, both initially and on a continuing basis, and for the supportive roles of diocesan officers. (1996, p. 64)

Within this dynamic and participative scenario:

The parish priest has the particular task of being a distributing focus for the ministry team and the whole church.

It remains one of the unresolved problems of the church how simultaneously to affirm the ministry of the rank and file of the local church and at the same time recognise the specifically essential work of the priest. (1996, p. 66)

This 'specifically essential work of the priest' is later described in terms of being:

the one who persuasively draws together and holds the values of their community. One metaphor for exploring the roles and qualities of priesthood required in one who presides, is to consider the process of discernment, blessing and witnessing. (1996, p. 71)

Thus the priest is seen in terms of one who *presides*, through overseeing the widest possible processes of discernment in the community:
• through exercising the skills of adult educators;
• through their own discipline of study;
• through being a link with the catholic church worldwide;
• through modelling reflective practice in ministry;
• through being not just a professional minister, but acknowledging his or her own struggles with the mysteries of salvation;

- through having a care for many issues great and small, and having a feel for the whole enterprise (this is the heart of the priest's tasks);
- through standing at the crossroads at the heart of the mission and eucharist of the people of God (this is why priests are set apart in a new relationship with God, the world, the church, and their friends);
- through enabling the liturgical performance of sacramental acts that are blessings;
- through not being on the front line of mission all the time, but more humbly assisting others to recognise their own ministries and potential for growth;
- through witnessing to the community beyond the church, and to those on its fringes.

He concludes, 'The parson-shaped hole in the parish will not go away. However, increasingly the priest's task will be to empower others to understand their vital role of witnessing to Christ in their own spheres of influence' (1996, p. 79).

However, it is the local church which 'focuses in one place the church's catholic and apostolic witness to the possibility of redeemed or true human society and a reconciled world'.

EXERCISE

How do you evaluate Greenwood's understanding of the role of the priest? Is he simply reinforcing the notion of the 'mono-minister' who is the one 'professional trained leader' and authoritative due to the exercise of these particular skills?

Is there a sense in which this recipe for sharing responsibilities for ministry in the local Christian community in fact becomes a recipe for even greater stress upon the ordained, and more controlled, individually negotiated participation by voluntary laity, or can you support Greenwood's vision more positively?

How accurate is it to say that 'the parson-shaped hole in the parish (or local church) will not go away'?　▶▶

How does this vision for the future relate to your reflections on
- the friars proclaiming *absolvere* in complex, plural urban culture;
- the issues about 'distance' in the story of Richard;
- the understanding of ministry and priesthood in *Pride and Prejudice*?

Wesley Carr

The second contemporary theologian to be considered is Wesley Carr, Dean of Westminster Abbey. He has written a number of books on ministry, including *Brief Encounters* (1985), *The Priestlike Task* (1985) and *The Pastor as Theologian* (1989). The ideas developed in this chapter are taken from his contribution to the workbook prepared for the Aston Training Scheme, under the title *Styles of Ministry and Priesthood*.

For Carr, writing about the Church of England:

> This church can never define itself from within: it cannot by itself decide what it is, how it will be ordered, and even exactly what it will believe. It will, of course, rightly try to do all those things. That is part of its continual examination of how faithful it is being to the foundations of the gospel. But it will also have to be pragmatic, recognising:
> 1) that what people believe is never known, even to them;
> 2) that the gospel is not just given, but always has to be grasped and interpreted;
> 3) that the church is never solely a gathering of the faithful but always a mix of belief and unbelief.
>
> When the church identifies itself as believers and others as non-believers it is merely defending itself against such richness. The Church of England cannot define itself from within. But neither can it simply be what other people expect or wish it to be. Many claim to know what the church ought to be and do. They are as frightening in the security of their ignorance as some Christians are in their apparent certainty.

Carr goes on to argue that 'church' is 'negotiated':

> Churches, like all institutions, are negotiated. They exist as they are created by the interaction between those who have an interest in them and those who make claims upon them. The Church of England dis-

tinctively addresses this fact with theological and organisational seriousness:

1) The theological seriousness is found in this church's traditional interest in the doctrine of the incarnation. Anglican scholars have made major contributions to its study, which is more about being than effectiveness. And the church's day to day life has been distinguished by attention to worship and liturgy and by a ministry that is present to all and as reliable as we can make it. This stance is founded on a profound grasp of the way in which God's being dwells with humankind. The incarnation is first about being, not achievement. It concerns the way in which God and humanity negotiate relations between them, both in the person of Jesus Christ and between him and men and women throughout time.

2) The organisational seriousness shows in the way that the church is structured to provide people, regardless of their allegiance, with opportunities to encounter God. Since such occasions cannot be planned, a certain amount of organisational untidiness inevitably marks the Church of England. But underneath the complexities lies a simple structure for a basic task. This church is always being created by negotiation between people with their expectation of God, the church or believers and those who claim some knowledge of that God.

This fact of negotiation has important consequences for notions of ministry:

If the Church of England exists through negotiation and not by definition, its ministers will be similarly defined. This is why the role of 'vicar' is supremely important. He or she represents a presence that is a recognised authority to know about and speak about God. Underneath an often jokey or casual exterior the expectations are very high. This frequently becomes apparent when things go wrong. The sense of being let down is acute. This is because the vicar is in people's minds, though not always consciously, the one who stands on the boundary between God and the world or between the church and themselves. The vicar is a boundary person, whom people use to help them define who they are in relation to God and to the church. In that sense the vicar is genuinely vicarious: he or she stands both on behalf of people and on behalf of God. However, we (and especially clergy) need clearly to grasp that all this is not a matter of fact. We are talking of feelings and beliefs that are often irrational or, at least, inexplicable. If ministers begin to believe that they manage people's actual relations with God, things go seriously wrong. Among the many reasons for the Reformation, for instance, one was a growing resistance to a church whose clergy laid claim to such power. The vicar's role as here described is part of that world of assumptions within which all ministers have to work. These are fundamental in people's lives; they also comprise that dimension to human life and experience to which the Church of England attends on distinctive theological grounds.

EXERCISE

'The incarnation is first about being, not achievement. It concerns the way in which God and humanity negotiate relations between them, both in the person of Jesus Christ, and between him and men and women ... ' What does this statement say to you about vocation and ministry?

Carr argues for the importance of the 'vicar' as one set apart (distance, as with Elisha) to enable an essential 'dependency', order and authority. Compare this idea with Greenwood's call for the priest or public minister to acknowledge their own vulnerability, and to identify deeply with the local church as its 'president'.

What are the features of 'that world of assumptions within which all ministers have to work'?

Dependency and interpretation

Carr goes on to explain that the key concept to understand this vision of the local church is that of 'dependency'. Miller's (1993, p. 106) study of the church's ministry, which as the language of this quotation shows did not emanate from within the church, came to this conclusion:

> The minister, as he goes about his job as a representative of the church on the boundary with the rest of society, has a great deal of hope invested in him. He is asked to show dependability and reassurance, while recognising at times that within the church and within himself there is much uncertainty and confusion ... This means that there is inevitably an element of childlike dependency in the relationship to

the church, and thus to its representatives, in that to some extent they are asked to solve the insoluble, cure the incurable, and make reality go away. Ministers of the church, therefore, have to receive this dependency. Sometimes they get stuck into a paternalistic posture; sometimes they are able to help their parishioners both to recognise dependency and discover their own resources and capabilities. But for the church the dependent posture is itself a reality that cannot be made to go away – without it the church as an institution can scarcely exist – so it is something to be constantly worked with.

Carr argues, however, that the term 'dependency' should not be misunderstood.

It is not used here to describe people in the pejorative sense of the word 'dependent'. Even less does it suggest what has come to be called 'a dependency culture' in which people are invited to surrender, or at least immobilise, their autonomy. The word is value neutral and describes the given nature of some relationships. For instance a child, however old he or she becomes, can be described as always dependent on his mother. As a baby that dependence is obvious and physical. As the child matures, he grows out of that style of dependence. But his mother remains in his mind and throughout his life he relies on that presence. Sometimes he is conscious of this; usually he is unaware of it: the reliance is unconscious. He is always in that sense dependent.

Christians should have few problems with the idea. The gospel invites us to depend on (have faith in) God, but not in such faith to surrender our responsibility for what God calls us to be and do. Nevertheless, the optimum relationship of faith is properly a dependent one. In this sense people look dependently to the church and to God. The church exists and its ministers work in that context.

The result is that people inside and outside of the formal church need authoritative figures to give focus and access to something profound about the Christian gospel.

Notions of 'collaborative ministry' may blur distinctions that are necessary for the total ministry of the church. Carr contends that:

First, ministry is about working with people. But people are varied, both in their needs and desires. If, therefore, the church is to continue to engage with people, not least in the complexity of today's world, its ministry needs to be as varied as possible, while remaining coherent. The church's working base is to provide as many access points to the gospel as possible. Historically this has been done by creating parishes and building churches. Noticeably, however, this approach has been less successful in the complex life of cities than in the more recognisable communities in rural areas. In today's mobile society in which people's imaginations are constantly stimulated by the pervasive media, the variety of access points is going to be more dynamic. The traditional provision of lay and ordained ministry remains remarkably suitable for this task, provided that we do not obscure it with temporary fads. For some purposes people need a believed authority: so they turn to the vicar as an authorised minister. For other purposes they may need what is felt to be a less formal, even more altruistic, point of contact. Here is the role of the lay person. He or she represents the unconditional availability of God in a way which is denied the ordained minister.

Second, all ministry is about engaging with people and interpreting fragments of their experience in the light of the gospel. Qualitatively there is little or no difference between the potential of lay and ordained. The distinction between them chiefly lies, as we might expect of a negotiated church, in other people's capacity to use ministers. Lay and ordained are not differentiated by learning, holiness, spirituality or status. But there is a difference that is determined by what we might call 'usability': how best can people find some access to God and an interpretation of their life that includes this transcendent dimension?

Third, a critical point of difference is the basis of that interpretation. From the perspective of the world, ordained ministers are expected to speak with the authority of the church. They are, therefore, assumed to know even things that cannot be known. Funerals are good occasions for theological testing. The question 'Will I see my parrot in heaven?' is not casually asked of the minister; he is expected to know. The Church of England, because of this demand, has emphasised that its ordained ministry is both learned and pastoral. It has emphasised training. The vicar's learning is not expected to be esoteric. He or she is learned in order to be pastoral. Neither learning nor pastoral skill can be thought of apart from the other. The contemporary church is the weaker because the links between theology and pastoral action have become loose. The minister is supposed to have a study so that he or she can be pastorally effective. It follows, too, as has been increasingly recognised through the church's investment in continuing ministerial education or in-service training, that such learning is never finally acquired. It is a quality that people rightly expect in the minister. Ministers, therefore, are expected to maintain their professional competence, which is always first the discipline of theology.

Fourth, the lay person can have a more relaxed engagement with people. He or she is not expected to know, although they may have a view. Lay people have a particular resource for ministry, namely their testimony. There is a classic exposition of such ministry in John 9, the story of the man born blind. He encounters Jesus, is healed and then testifies powerfully on the basis of that encounter and his ignorance: 'I do not know.'

Fifth, such different ministries are not well described as collaborative. The ordained minister does not enable the laity: they are already enabled by God and by being immersed in his world. Thinking about ministry in this light leads us to the idea of its being complementary. The church acknowledges that those with whom it ministers have freedom to decide how they receive such ministry. For some purposes they will turn to the authority of order; for others, the authority of experience. The variety of access and response is part of the richness of Christ's ministry in his world. There is no competition between lay and ordained but complementarity. Such an approach also gives the lie to any sense that lay ministry is a substitute for either inadequate clergy or insufficient ordained people.

Another aspect of the fact that ministry is about 'negotiation' is that:

instead of trying to achieve everything, the minister has to recognise that their ministry will consist of dealing with fragments of people's lives, or moments of significance more than with long term relationships: such ministry is one of interpretation.

EXERCISE
How might you best deploy the word 'collaborative' in relation to your understanding of ministry?

How do you evaluate Carr's distinctions between lay and ordained ministry?   ▶▶

In what ways might Catholic and Reformed churches have a different approach to Carr's description in Anglicanism of the 'negotiation' that underlies Christian ministry?

What is the significance of seeing ministry in terms of 'fragments and moments'? What are the dangers?

How does Carr's advocacy of a future scenario for ministry relate to your reflections on:
• women and ministry, particularly notions about motherhood and the authority of self-effacement;
• issues about order and authority, local and catholic;
• Underhill's ideas about spirituality and ministry;
• the respective roles of amateur and professional?

To the extent that ministry is about 'interpretation', what resources are required for this task?

EXERCISE
📖 **Read Ephesians 4.**

Make notes of your reflections in relation to 'ministry tomorrow'.

Here are some features of the passage for consideration:
• 'There is one body and one spirit ... but grace was given to each of us according to the measure of Christ's gift': a dynamic between oneness and variety is part of creation, and of the life of the church;
• unity and maturity are part of the call or vocation of each constituent part;
• Christ is the head of the body, which is built up in love;
• Christians, as members of this developing body, will be distinctive in the world, in lifestyle, values and aspirations;
• we develop by 'speaking truth with our neighbour', comparing independent testimonies; oneness has to be negotiated as well as received;

- all our efforts should be for the edification of the whole; the oneness of the body of Christ is prior to the particularity of its parts;
- forgiveness, *absolvere*, is the way in which the Christian journey proceeds;
- in chapter 3 verse 7 Paul explains, 'Of this gospel I was made a minister according to the gift of God's grace which was given me by the working of his power.'

EXERCISE
📖 **Re-read Ephesians 4.**

How does this passage influence ideas of ministry?

What do you think?

Here are some further issues for consideration:

1. Look at your answers to questions 1, 2, 9 and 10 in the Ministry Questionnaire. Make notes of your reflections in the light of this chapter.
2. At this stage of your study, how would you complete the sentence: 'Ministry is ... '?
3. Write a paper for the members of your church on 'The shape and style of Christian ministry for the twenty-first century'.

Further reading

Carr, W (1985), *Brief Encounters: pastoral ministry through the occasional offices*, London, SPCK.

Carr, W (1985), *The Priestlike Task: a model for developing and training the church's ministry*, London, SPCK.

Carr, W (1989), *The Pastor as Theologian: the integration of pastoral ministry, theology and discipleship*, London, SPCK.

Carr, W (1997), *Handbook of Pastoral Studies: learning and practising Christian ministry*, London, SPCK.

Goodliff, P (1998), *Care in a Confused Climate*, London, Darton, Longman and Todd.

Greenwood, R (1994), *Transforming Priesthood*, London, SPCK.

Greenwood, R (1996), *Practising Community: the tasks of the local church*, London, SPCK.

Heeney, D (1998), *Motivating Your Parish To Change*, San Jose, California, Resource Publications.

Moody, C (1992), *Eccentric Ministry*, London, Darton, Longman and Todd.

Morisy, A (1997), *Beyond the Good Samaritan*, London, Mowbray.

REFERENCES

Advisory Council for the Church's Ministry (1987), *Education for the Church's Ministry: occasional paper 22*, London, ACCM.

Allen, R (1912), *Mission Methods: St Paul's or Ours?*, London, Robert Scott.

Allen, R (1927), *The Spontaneous Expansion of the Church and the Causes which Hinder it*, London, World Dominion Press.

Allen, R (1930), *The Case for the Voluntary Clergy*, London, Eyre and Spottiswoode.

Archbishop of Canterbury's Commission on Urban Priority Areas (1985), *Faith in the City*, London, Church House Publishing.

Carr, W (1985a), *Brief Encounters: pastoral ministry through the occasional offices*, London, SPCK.

Carr, W (1985b), *The Priestlike Task: a model for developing and training the church's ministry*, London, SPCK.

Carr, W (1989), *The Pastor as Theologian: the integration of pastoral ministry, theology and discipleship*, London, SPCK.

Carr, W (1992), *Say One for Me*, London, SPCK.

Church of England (1998), *Common Worship: initiation services*, London, Church House Publishing.

Collinson, P (1990), The Late Medieval Church and its Reformation 1400–1600, in J McManners (ed.), *The Oxford Illustrated History of Christianity*, Oxford University Press.

Council for Christian Unity (1993), *Together in Mission and Ministry: the Porvoo Common Statement with essays on church and ministry in Northern Europe*, London, Church House Publishing.

Cropper, M (1958), *Evelyn Underhill*, London, Longmans, Green and Co.

Fletcher, S (1989), *Maude Royden: a life*, Oxford, Blackwell.

Forster, M (1984), *Significant Sisters*, Oxford, Oxford University Press.

General Synod Board of Education (1985), *All are Called: towards a theology of the laity*, London, Church Information Office Publishing.

Gore, C (1891), *The Incarnation of the Son of God: the Bampton lectures for 1891*, London, John Murray.

Gore, C (1901), *The Body of Christ*, London, John Murray.

Gore, C (1905), *Roman Catholic Claims*, London, Longmans, Green and Co.

Gore, C (1926), *The Reconstruction of Belief*, London, John Murray.

Gore, C (1929), *Jesus of Nazareth*, London, Home University Library.

Greene, G (1971), *The Power and the Glory*, London, Heinemann and Bodley Head.

Greenwood, R (1994), *Transforming Priesthood*, London, SPCK.

Greenwood, R (1996), *Practising Community: the tasks of the local church*, London, SPCK.

McGinn, B (1998), *The Flowering of Mysticism*, New York, Crossway Publishing.

Melinsky, H (1992), *The Shape of the Ministry*, Norwich, Canterbury Press.

Miller, E J (1993), *From Dependency to Autonomy: studies in organisation and change*, London, Free Association Books.

Mitchell, B (1982), *Mission and Ministry*, Wilmington, Michael Glazier.

Richardson, A and Bowden, J (ed.) (1983), *A New Dictionary of Christian Theology*, London, SCM.

Royden, M (1924), *The Church and Woman*, London, James Clarke and Co.

Schillebeeckx, E (1980), The right of the community to a priest, *Concilium*, 133, 95–135.

Schillebeeckx, E (1981), *Ministry: a case for change*, London, SCM.

Schleiermacher, F (1967), *Christmas Eve: dialogue on the incarnation*, Louisville, Kentucky, John Knox Press.

Underhill, E (1907), *The Lost World*, London, Heinemann.

Underhill, E (1911), *Mysticism*, London, Methuen.

Underhill, E (1936), *Worship*, London, James Nisbet and Co.

Underhill, E (1937), *The Spiritual Life*, London, Hodder and Stoughton.

Underhill, E (1946), *Collected Papers*, London, Longmans, Green and Co.

Underhill, E (1947), *Concerning the Inner Life with The House of the Soul*, London, Methuen.

APPENDIX: Ministry Questionnnaire

1. How would you describe your local church?

2. What do you think that the church is for?

3. (a) Consult the following list:
   - put a tick by the three most important functions of a local church
   - put a cross by the three least important functions of a local church
   - underline any that should be the particular responsibility of the clergy

   helping the sick and needy
   prayer
   converting people to become Christians
   worship of God
   teaching about Jesus
   doing baptisms, weddings and funerals
   creating a sense of community
   working with the poor and unemployed
   promoting youth clubs and uniformed organisations
   being there
   raising money
   witnessing to an alternative form of society
   challenging sin and sinners
   celebrating the eucharist
   making a nourishing fellowship
   teaching young people and upholding family life
   helping people in the world of work

maintaining a special building
supporting mission

3. (b) What important functions are missing from this list?

3. (c) Name three things that concern people in your community.
How, if at all, does the church share in these concerns?

4. What do you understand by the following terms?

Vicar
Minister
Reader
PCC
Non Stipendiary Minister
Synod
Bishop
Parish
Ordained Local Minister
Deacon
Priest
Churchwarden
Elder
Pastoral Visitor

5. Why are people ordained to be priests and ministers?

6. How, if at all, should clergy be different:
   • from other Christians?
   • from other people in the community?

7. Should the priest, vicar or minister be chosen from local church
members, or come from outside? Why?

8. What do you think about the place of:
   • women in the church?
   • men in the church?
   • children and young people in the church?

9. What, if any, changes would you like to see in the way that the church is organised?

10. How do you use your local church and your local clergy?

Applying for the Church Colleges' Certificate Programme

The certificate programme is available in Anglican Church Colleges of Higher Education throughout England and Wales. There are currently hundreds of students on this programme, many with no previous experience of study of this kind. There are no entry requirements. Some people choose to take Certificate courses for their own interest and personal growth, others take these courses as part of their training for ministry in the church. Some go on to complete the optional assignments and, after the successful completion of three courses, gain the Certificate. Courses available through the *Exploring Faith: theology for life* series are ideal for establishing ability and potential for studying theology and biblical studies at degree level, and they provide credit onto degree programmes.

For further details of the Church Colleges' Certificate Programme, related to this series, please contact the person responsible for Adult Education in your local diocese or one of the colleges at the addresses provided:

The Administrator of Part-time Programmes, Department of Theology and Religious Studies, Chester College, Parkgate Road, CHESTER, CH1 4BJ ☎ 01244 375444

The Registry, Roehampton Institute, Froebel College, Roehampton Lane, LONDON, SW15 5PJ ☎ 0181 392 3087

The Registry, Canterbury Christ Church University College, North Holmes Road, CANTERBURY, CT1 1QU ☎ 01227 767700

The Registry, College of St Mark and St John, Derriford Road, PLYMOUTH, PL6 8BH ☎ 01752 636892

The Registry, Trinity College, CARMARTHEN, Carmarthenshire, SA31 3EP ☎ 01267 676804 (direct)

Church Colleges' Programme, The Registry, King Alfred's College, Sparkford Road, WINCHESTER, SO22 4NR ☎ 01962 841515

Part-time Programmes, The Registry, College of St Martin, Bowerham Road, LANCASTER, LA1 3JD ☎ 01524 384529